Wisdom Stories
of
Nine Women

W. Wayne Price

Illustrated by Susan Nagy

Wisdom Stories of Nine Women
ISBN: Softcover 978-1-949888-35-5
Copyright © 2017 by W. Wayne Price

All rights reserved. No part of this book may be reproduced or transmitted in any form or by any means, electronic or mechanical, including photocopying, recording, or by any information storage and retrieval system, without permission in writing from the publisher.

Illustrated by Susan Nagy who is a Yorktown, Virginia Artist.

To order additional copies of this book, contact:

Parson's Porch Books
1-423-475-7308
www.parsonsporch.com

Parson's Porch Books is an imprint of **Parson's Porch & Book Publishers** in Cleveland, Tennessee, which has double focus. We focus on the needs of creative writers who need a professional publisher to get their work to market, **&** we also focus on the needs of others by sharing our profits with those who struggle in poverty to meet their basic needs of food, clothing, shelter and safety.

Dedicated to Portia and Jessica, our two daughters, who have given us love, joy, and wholeness on this journey we call life.

Introduction

W. Wayne Price answered a definite call to the ministry at age fifteen. He was ordained at age nineteen. He was active in his church as a young boy and teenager.

He was often tasked with getting his five younger siblings ready for church on Sunday mornings. When he was a sophomore in college, he was called to pastor a small mountain church in Pruden, Tennessee. He held this position for two years. During his senior year in college, he did not pastor a church, and he was miserable.

Three months after our marriage in 1960, the Baptist Associational Minister in east Tennessee asked him to take a small part-time church while he was teaching junior high school English and waiting for me to graduate college. We moved from our apartment about twelve miles from Carson-Newman College in Jefferson City in Jefferson City, Tennessee to the Dumplin Baptist Church in New Market, Tennessee. We moved into a large one-room schoolhouse that the church had renovated into a parsonage. We had been living in a furnished apartment. The church provided the basics, and we lived there for almost two years.

We left Dumplin Baptist Church to move into a small house in Middletown, Kentucky, I taught high school French and English while Wayne attended Southern Baptist Theological Seminary in Louisville, Kentucky. During the Fall of his first year of seminary, we were contacted by Union Baptist Church in Defoe, Kentucky. We were there for five years:

1963 - 1968. Meanwhile, Wayne graduated from Southern Baptist Theological Seminary in 1965. He was not yet ready to assume the duties of a full-time congregation, so we both enrolled as graduate students at the University David's of Kentucky. He stopped just short of writing a Ph.D. dissertation in English. He was called in 1968 to pastor his first full-time church - David's Fork Baptist Church in Lexington, Kentucky. We spent three wonderful years there. The church and parsonage were in a beautiful rural area. My father came to live with us after my mother's death; he enjoyed watching the sheep and cattle in the field just across the road from the parsonage. Our first daughter, Portia, was born while we were there. The church members adopted her as "their baby."

After almost three years there, a pulpit search committee from First Baptist Church in Winchester, Kentucky (twelve miles from the David's Fork Church), approached Wayne about becoming their minister. We were sad to leave David's Fork, but First Baptist was in a county-seat town and had 1100 members. Our second daughter, Jessica, was born there, and she became that church's adopted baby. While there, I taught at a junior college and a pre-school for children with special needs. I stayed at the University long enough to graduate with a Ph.D. in French Language and Literature. We had a good ministry in a good church for almost ten and one-half years.

At that time, one of our church members moved to Williamsburg, Virginia. One day he called to tell us that the senior minister of the Williamsburg Baptist Church had announced his retirement after twenty-nine years there. Our friend thought it would be a perfect fit for Wayne. After visiting the church while on vacation. shortly after that Wayne was being interviewed by their pulpit search committee. We moved to Williamsburg in January, 1981.

We were very happy to be on the East Coast after pastoring three Kentucky churches. Wayne was senior minister of the Williamsburg Baptist Church for seventeen and one-half years. We loved living in a college town that also provided knowledge of some of the beginnings of American history. We took advantage of all that we could see and do. The girls enjoyed our time there. They made friends and were involved in several activities. I decided to change careers (at God's calling) to become a Licensed Professional Counselor. I attended the College of William and Mary part-time for five years and received my counseling license in December, 1988. I have worked as a psychotherapist since that time.

Wayne also made a great change in his life in 1998. He felt called to the Episcopal priesthood, so he took one year to study for the General Ordination Exams. He was first ordained as a Deacon, and six months later was ordained to the Episcopal priesthood. He accepted a position as assistant to the rector at Grace Episcopal Church, Yorktown, Virginia. He enjoyed working with the priest there very much until he retired due to illness in 2006. He was then able to focus on completing these short stories that he had been compiling for over ten years. I had the stories professionally edited by my friend, Carla Jones several years ago. Now I have finally fulfilled Wayne's request that I have then published for him posthumously. I am very grateful to

David Russell Tullock, who told me that it would be an honor for him to publish this collection. I believe that God put him in my path at just the right time. We hope that you will enjoy these vignettes, as they are composites of women that Wayne ministered to during his forty-seven years of ministry. He has given us much in these stories that are charming, humorous, and insightful. Thank you, my dear Wayne, for sharing your gifts with the world.

Jo Anna Price-Hoppe, LPC, LMFT
February 20, 2017

AGNES

"I've been coming to see you now for three months! I'm sixty-seven years old today, and I never thought I'd need a professional counselor. But then, I've never been so confused or indecisive."

"Happy birthday, Agnes," Diana said with a warm smile. "Haven't we talked about confusion being a starting point for examining our thoughts and feelings?"

Agnes glanced around the office. It had been arranged to be a comfortable place. A desk, a small sofa, a rocking chair, the usual computer and telephone, an array of framed diplomas and certifications hung on the wall with a single window. With its sky-blue walls, the room was comfortable and cozy with of some of Diana's family pictures and a few stuffed animals placed around the room.

"You've gotten to be like a friend to me—not the kind of going-out-to-lunch kind of friend, and I guess in your work you can't do that anyway. But even when I'm not here, I think about my situation just like I do when you are here listening to me."

"A lot happens between therapy sessions. I'm glad to hear that you take something with you," Diana said.

"Even though we've been over this before, I need to think about it out loud, all of it from the beginning. Maybe because it's my birthday; maybe it's because I have to come to a decision. Diana, I need to talk, and you listen so well."

"Thank you, Agnes. I'm here to listen. Please continue."

A long pause with only the muted sound of the ticking clock. Agnes chuckled and then continued rather wistfully.

"Walt left me twelve years ago. Alone at age fifty-five! He said he just didn't want to be married anymore. Almost thirty years together, and then he was gone. Just gone. Ours was hardly a perfect marriage, but I suppose its biggest flaw was routine, which led to boredom, and then apathy. I knew it was like that, but we had simply gotten comfortable, and I thought neither of us wanted to make any waves. Work, church, some close social friends, the house, and yard responsibilities—we were busy with a kind of day-to-day sameness, without any real passion or excitement about life. But we were both in it for the long haul, or so I thought. I've often tried to decide exactly what went wrong, blaming myself, trying to deal with the shame of failure. I've even entertained the idea that I wanted out of the marriage as much as Walt did; maybe I just didn't have the courage to do anything about it. You know, the devil you know is better than the devil you don't know."

"Indeed!" Diana agreed.

"We didn't have any children, so dividing things up proved relatively easy, except of course for the emotional strain. I still had my job, and the stability that provided gave me a kind of escape hatch. But it was the nights! Rambling about that big old house! Empty, empty, empty! Do you have any idea how many strange sounds you hear in a big old house at night?"

"Not really, Agnes. I've never lived alone. Tell me about those nights."

"Well, I guess I was more aware of night sounds since I was alone. Every bump or creak or animal noise from outside seemed much louder and more threatening since I was there by myself. It's amazing the difference just having someone else in the house with you can make. I wasn't alone when Walt was there, but I have decided, however, that I was lonely long before he left. Yes, I had and still have a fair number of friends, and a few very close friends. I have some relatives nearby. However none of them could take the place of a husband, someone to share my life with. And since Walt left, nothing any of them has said or done much to take away my sense of shame, my emptiness, my confusion. Most of my friends and family were furious with Walt, and I suppose I was too, but I was too busy blaming myself to hold him accountable for his faults. He is a good man. But that's all water over the dam."

"Sometimes good things come out of bad situations, Agnes."

"And that happened to me. I tried to make a new life for myself. I think I've done pretty well."

Agnes paused, looked out the window and noticed the sprinkle of rain and shafts of sunlight.

"Kind of like outside. Raining and sunshiny at the same time. I did all the "widow" things since that's what I felt like. Church, lunch with the girls, day trips, a reading club, an occasional craft class. I got so I valued my independence, enjoyed being on my own instead of identifying myself mostly as somebody's wife. But I never could deal very well with the nighttime. I still don't know if I missed the routine of his presence, the physical contact— limited though it was at the end, or just the idea of somebody to call my own. Since I couldn't figure it out, I just put one foot in front of the other and kept on going. I seemed to feel increasingly content, but hardly happy. I refused to admit the unhappy part.

"Almost a year ago, everything changed again. Frank happened! We met at Sally's dinner party. An obvious set-up, but then I saw Frank again at church. He invited me to dinner and a movie. Soon we found ourselves doing something once a week, and then talking on the phone in the middle of the week.

"Frank is a delight. Not exactly handsome, but attractive. He challenges me to think more deeply, and his kindness to other people and to me sometimes makes me wonder if he is for real! At first, I was flattered by his attention, but I don't think I felt much sexual attraction; I suppose I had put my sexuality in some trunk of memories. Frank primarily filled some of the emptiness and loneliness I felt because we did things together and talked a lot."

"So, Frank filled some empty spaces in your life."

"Exactly! And bit by bit I realized where my former emptiness came from: I had not realized the importance of having someone care about me and having someone to care for. The more time Frank and I spent together, the more I understood my need for both his casual presence and those flashes of intensity in our conversations, even the excitement of our disagreements about ideas. Frank brought back to life some of the fullness I had lost over the years of my marriage to Walt, some of what I may have known was missing but wouldn't admit when he left."

"So, your realizations about caring and being cared for came rather slowly?" Diana asked.

"Well, yes, and I finally came to the point of admitting it. In fact, that admission frightened me. It made me wonder if I had passed some emotional point of no return. That was just before I called to make my first appointment with you. When I felt that enthusiasm inside, always when I was with Frank, it was so good on the one hand and so strange on the other hand that I think I had forgotten what to do with mixed feelings. But this is the part of the story I haven't told you.

"Almost every time we were together after the first two or three months, Frank would give me a peck on the cheek as he left, sometimes a polite hug. I didn't read too much into this since most of my friends exchange these little greetings and farewells. Then one night at my front door, he took me into his arms and just held me for a long time.

"All sorts of fireworks went off. I felt him harden against me and then the tingling in my own self. I think I had forgotten what all of that felt like—both physically and emotionally. In fact, I felt faint. Finally, Frank said, 'It's getting more and more difficult to leave you.' I didn't know what to say, but I knew I didn't want him to let me go."

"Were you able to respond to him?" Diana asked.

"You mean, what did I say? Well, nothing at first. He was looking at me like he was waiting for me to make some reply. Finally, I told him that I was surprised, confused, and needed time to think about what that meant. And then I said we would have a lot to talk about. Then he kissed me, full and long. I started to cry, just buried my face in his shoulder and stood there. I don't remember ever feeling that way before."

"Even in your younger years?"

"Maybe when I was a teenager, or in my early twenties. Then, you feel all sorts of sexual power, but there is no long experience to give it deep meaning. You think so, I thought so, and you only imagine a little bit of its implications. When you are old enough to see the possibility of the end of your own life, and you weigh that with decades of experience, both good and bad, that kind of closeness takes on a life of its own.

"There in my own hallway, by the door of a multitude of comings and goings, I experienced something absolutely new. Whatever it was washed over me with great fear and ecstatic excitement. I must have stood there in Frank's arms crying for a long time. He never questioned me or apologized; I felt like he knew exactly why I was crying—even though I didn't. In that short span of time, I realized that I didn't want him to leave either."

"Were you able to tell Frank this?"

"Yes, I assured him that I was all right but that I needed some time to process all those mixed-up feelings. So then began some serious conversations, which included some exchange of the most intimate and personal parts of our life stories.

"As it turns out, Frank is hardly perfect. He had not been nearly so attentive to his wife and sons. By the time his wife died, their relationship was no better than mine and Walt's. But Frank accepted and admitted most of the fault. He had been absorbed in his work, had made money and lost money, but the work itself proved to be his obsession. His sons are grown now, and though they get along, they don't share much in common. I suppose you could say that Frank and I are alike that way – we're both slow learners, but we are making progress. We also shared a kind of non-specific sadness; maybe that was part of the initial attraction. But after the night at my front door, the sadness began to give way. Our friends teased us about our silliness, our playfulness, and our laughter that hadn't been there before, and I could tell they were happy, and even a bit relieved, to see the changes in both of us."

"You were becoming more aware of how much you enjoyed each other?" Diana asked.

"Yes, as we saw each other more in the weeks and months that followed, we began to talk about our future, and it became clear to both of us that we wanted to be married. We became increasingly intimate physically. The process was almost funny—two senior citizens with adolescent sexual urges and equally adolescent awkwardness. It was almost like neither of us knew what we were doing, how to respond, what to say. I think we kind of laughed our way through the early efforts, but, oh my! —how we settled in to some of the most satisfying experiences of my life."

"Good for you, Agnes!"

"Frank has never stayed overnight, and yet I don't think either of us has any guilt about our sexual relationship. I try not to get caught in trying to figure out that inconsistency."

Agnes looked out the window and noticed that the sun had gone and the rain was falling more heavily.

"The weather seems to be following my story," she added with another chuckle.

Diana looked out the window and nodded. She seemed to anticipate some conflict lurking in the background, now about to come center stage. Some kind of hard rain was falling within her client.

"Here's the rub," Agnes continued. "We want to be married, but a money issue will make my life much less comfortable than it is now. When Walt left, I received everything except his retirement, which was substantial. I got the house and furnishings, my car, and a rather significant savings. Well, I really didn't get the savings. It was placed in trust, the income of which comes to me as long as I live, and then it reverts to Walt's college. If I remarry, however, I no longer receive any money from the trust. I don't think Walt meant that to be a punishment; he probably figured that if I married, I would no longer need it, and the money could help needy students. I had no reason to question the terms of the trust because I had no interest in another marriage, at least at that time, and no expectations that I ever would."

"You couldn't have imagined then how dramatically those feelings could change?" Diana ventured.

"You're right," Agnes agreed. "I thought that I would never have any interest in remarrying. Now I realize that if I lose the trust income, I will have only Social Security, a small pension of my own, and the little bit I have managed to save these years since Walt left. Frank, unfortunately, has no property of his own and only a modest income from Social Security and a small pension."

"Could the two of you get by on the income you described?" Diana asked.

"Yes. I would have to sell my house and my lifestyle would be severely downsized, but we could make it. And Frank already lives much more simply than I do anyway."

"Agnes, Frank sounds like someone you could live more simply with."

"I'm sure you're right, Diana. I probably sound like a spoiled old lady who wants to have her cake and eat it too, but it isn't that clear cut. I said that when Walt left, I felt alone and empty. I also was afraid. Could I manage alone? The house and yard, the business decisions, the bills all overwhelmed me. I discovered, however, that I was better off than I had thought I could be. I had plenty to live on and discovered that I can manage my life alone quite well. Now, the issue seems to me to be less that of a selfish woman pulled between money and love, and more an issue of an insecure woman with a vivid memory of being alone with the consolation of a comfortable bank account."

"You took the words right out of my mouth," Diana replied.

Agnes smiled weakly, but she was obviously sad, near tears. She sat in silence, staring off out the rain-drenched window. Diana leaned forward and placed her hand on Agnes's folded hands. She said nothing; she waited with and for Agnes.

After a few moments, Agnes continued. "I suppose you wonder where Frank stands in all this. He knows everything I've told you. He wants to marry me regardless of our financial situation. Sometimes I think he understands my insecurity; at other times, I think he believes I should be able to trust him and our love for each other enough to let go of the money. He has made money and lost it and made it again and lost it again. Somehow it seems easier for him than it is for me."

"Agnes, maybe it is easier for Frank," Diana said

"This has become a really serious ethical dilemma. If we choose not to marry because of the trust, we could live together and be husband and wife in every way except the ceremony and the certificate. Frank would rather not do it that way, and I simply can't. I believe very deeply in the high place of the covenant between two people. Ironic, isn't it? I'm willing to risk the commitment of marriage even after a failed relationship, but I'm so afraid to risk letting go of financial security!"

Diana smiled in silent agreement as Agnes continued.

"We have talked often about our relationship if we do not marry and if we do not live together outside of marriage.

Would it survive? Frank has insisted that the decision is mine and that he will be with me as we are now if that is all he can have. I'm overwhelmed by his love and loyalty. I can't imagine, though, how the relationship could be sustained with Frank knowing that I refused to put marriage ahead of money, if I am unable to allow him to provide some of the security I need. Yet he says he is willing to live with that arrangement."

"The issue, Agnes, seems to be what you are willing and able to live with."

"What will I do? Frank isn't pushing me to decide, but I dislike this dilemma, this limbo. I could go on as I am, as we are. But I fear the creeping apathy that drained the life out of my marriage to Walt. Would it be better for both of us to end the relationship now and save even worse heartache later?"

"What do you honestly think and feel, Agnes?" Diana asked.

Agnes began to cry, first a lone tear from each eye and then a steady stream. She took a handful of tissues and sat quietly in the throes of her decision. Diana sat in a kind of reverent silence. After several minutes, Agnes looked at her watch, apologized for going past the hour, and made an appointment for the same time next week. They stood together and embraced. Agnes smiled as she slipped quietly out of the office.

RUTH

"Allie, no ride! You know Dad's gone, and I can't drive. Now move over and let me see if I can find those papers Will needs."

Allie scrambled into the back, her head pushed forward between the two front seats, tongue out, panting with excitement.

"I never saw such an animal! Most dogs love to chase cars. You'd rather ride in them. Well, let's see where those papers could be."

Ruth rummaged through the glove box: tire gauge, ice scraper, road maps.

"No need to bark, Allie. I told you we aren't going anywhere. Just got to get those papers."

Ruth felt the tears start to flow again.

"Now I've done it again. Can't seem to get through the simplest things without crying."

Finding some old restaurant napkins, Ruth blew her nose and wiped the tears. She leaned forward, over the open glove compartment, until her forehead rested on the dashboard. Allie nudged her arm as if to offer consolation. Finally, Ruth leaned back in the seat, right hand with napkins to her eyes, and reached her left hand around the neck of her Sheltie.

"You're the best friend in the world, Allie. We still have to find those papers and go back inside. There are just too many memories in this garage. Here it is, a folder from the dealer. They must be in here. We'll just take the whole thing with us, and Will can take what he needs."

Ruth replaced the contents of the glove box and climbed out of the car, but Allie didn't move.

"Come on, Allie! Back in the house! Allie, hurry up! Don't just sit there staring. You know I can't drive, and we aren't going anywhere."

She placed the folder on top of the car, leaned back inside, and gently tugged on Allie's collar to encourage her to cooperate. Allie reluctantly jumped out of the car. Ruth collected the folder, closed the car door, and returned to the house with Allie following close behind. They entered the den, which was two steps up from the garage. Still blotting her tears, Ruth closed the door behind Allie and walked to the overstuffed recliner. Allie settled at Ruth's feet.

They sat together for a long time, until they were family brought quickly into the present by the telephone. Ruth picked up the receiver from the end table beside the chair.

"Hello?" Ruth answered with more of a waver in her voice than she had expected.

"Hi, Mom. Are you all right?" said Will on the phone.

"Hi, son. I'm all right. I cry a lot, but I'm allowed to cry. It's only been two weeks. Mabel drives me to the store and to church, and the neighbors have been checking on me. Sometimes I feel almost helpless with everybody fussing over me."

"I'm glad your friends are looking out for you. Have you had a chance to find those car papers I'll need when we go to the DMV tomorrow?"

"Allie and I were just in the garage looking for them. I must have what you need—I pulled the entire folder of papers from the glove box, but I haven't gone through them yet. I'm sure what you need is there. Your dad kept all those things in the car, even the little notebook with all the dates for keeping the car in good repair. You can look through it when you get here tomorrow."

"Great, Mom. I think I can be there by about two o'clock."

"Two o'clock? Since Billy will be finished with kindergarten, maybe you could bring him along. He and I can visit while you go to the DMV."

"But Mom, you've got to go with me and sign the papers," Will said, a bit frustrated. He thought they had been over this.

"Why do I have to go? I'll just write a letter and authorize you to change the name on those papers. You know I don't like to stand in line."

"I don't think that'll work, and I don't want to have to make two trips. You should plan to go along."

"Well, Billy and I can both go then. When we get back, I'll fix us all a good dinner."

"Sounds like too much trouble for you."

Ruth changed the subject by asking, "Mary okay?"

"Yes, she's fine. She'll be studying for her nursing exam tomorrow while Billy and I are with you."

"Tell her I'm proud of her. She's the best daughter-in-law I've got." "And the only one you've got, Mom. I've got to go, but I'll see you tomorrow. Love you."

"I love you, too, son. And I'm glad you're just an hour away. I appreciate your help. Hug Billy for me. Bye, bye."

Ruth hung up the phone and went into the kitchen. At the refrigerator, she opened the door and eyed each shelf as if looking for something and then closed the door without taking anything out. Allie walked in from the den and looked at Ruth.

"Nothing tastes good, Allie. I just don't like to eat by myself. Never knew how much mealtimes depended on other folks. 'Best Cook in the Church', everybody says; now I can't even eat my own cooking! Guess that's natural. Forty-one years Dad and I ate together, talked and laughed through nearly every meal. How is somebody your whole world one day and just gone the next?"

Ruth sat on the counter stool, pulled a tissue from the box, and wiped her eyes again.

"How about a walk, Allie? Fresh air will do us both a world of good."

Hearing the word "walk," Allie ran to the pantry, nudged the door open, and pulled the leash from the closet hook. She followed Ruth to the hall closet and waited patiently until she put on her coat and gloves. Ruth bent down and fastened the leash, and the two of them went out the front door and down the four steps to the walk and driveway.

* * *

Ruth handed Allie a crust of toast and carried her cup and cereal bowl to the sink.

"You had a good time with Billy yesterday, didn't you Allie? He looks exactly like his dad at that age. It's almost like watching Will grow up again. Such a sweet boy, and so smart, too. Bet you would like to have him around all the time."

Allie sat watching Ruth and cocked her head as if to answer, "Yes!"

"I would, too. But we can be glad they live close by. Once a week is not enough, but they live a lot closer than Mabel's children."

Ruth remembered that the light bulb in the floor lamp in the den had burned out when she tried to turn it on.

"I need to change that light bulb, Allie. Let's go to the garage and get a new one."

Ruth walked to the door to the garage with Allie following close behind and opened it. Before Ruth could take a step into the garage, Allie rushed past her and started barking at the driver's side door of the car.

"Allie, we've been through this. I don't know how to drive. I wish I did. I'm already tired of depending on Mabel, even if she is my best friend. I never thought I'd need to learn how to drive. I could still learn, but I don't feel very confident about anything these days. All I do is cry! Anyway, let's get that light bulb."

Leaving Allie beside the car, Ruth walked to the wall cabinet and examined the neat rows of household items. She located a sixty-watt bulb and started back to the door. Allie barked and wagged her tail.

"Sorry, Allie," said Ruth, a bit sadly as she opened the door to the den.

Allie faced the car door and barked again.

"Oh, I suppose it won't hurt to let you sit in the car."

Ruth opened the car door, and Allie hit the driver's seat with one clean jump, bounced over to the passenger side, and sat upright facing the windshield as if she were ready to begin a great adventure. But there was no driver. Allie gave an enthusiastic bark. Light bulb in one hand, the other hand on her hip, Ruth watched Allie.

"That's enough, girl. Come on."

But Allie didn't move; she just barked again.

"Just sit there then; I'll take the garbage can out to the curb."

Ruth placed the new light bulb on top of the car, pressed the button

for the electric garage door opener, and as the door jerked its way to the top, she tilted the garbage can and wheeled it toward the street. When Ruth returned to the garage, Allie was still planted in her seat. Ruth eased into the driver's seat ready to pull Allie out of the car, but she paused, placed her hands on the steering wheel, and began to cry. She pulled a tissue from her pocket.

"Allie, I don't know if I'm crying because Dad is gone, or because I feel so helpless. I thought he'd always be here. I don't know anything about money or taxes or cars or insurance or the bills. Will has to do it all while I sit and cry."

Ruth looked up and out the windshield. She had an idea.

"I could drive this car, couldn't I, Allie? Dad always said it almost drives itself. Stay right there, Allie. I'll be right back."

Ruth practically ran up the two steps to the den and disappeared into the house. Moments later, she returned with a set of keys.

"Let's see which one works."

She tried one unsuccessfully; the second one fit in the ignition. "Ah yes! Now let's see. I think all I need to do is turn it."

Ruth turned the key and the engine turned over, but there was a grinding sound because she didn't know she needed to let the key go. The strange noise startled Ruth into releasing the key; the engine purred. Ruth sat with her hands on the steering wheel, bracing herself as though expecting the car to shoot through the back of the garage, but it didn't move. Allie did, however. She barked with exhilaration and Ruth smiled.

"Now what am I going to do, Allie? I haven't the faintest idea! The best thing we can both do is stop this foolishness and get out of this car!"

She turned the key in the opposite direction, breathed a sigh of relief, and struggled to get the key from the ignition. She got out of the car, motioned to a puzzled Allie and climbed the two steps to the den.

Once inside, Ruth remembered that she didn't close the car door or the garage door. She returned to the garage, closed both doors, picked up the light bulb, and made her way back to the den, where the phone was ringing.

"Hello?"

"Hello, Ruth. It's Mabel. Ready to go to the store?"

"Hi, Mabel. Will and Billy came down yesterday. We went to the DMV and then stopped by the store on the way home. I thought I'd give you a day off."

"All right. In that case, would you like to go out to dinner tonight?" "Thanks, Mabel, but I don't think so. Why don't you come over and eat with me? I'll fix something simple, and we can just visit."

"That sounds good. Thanks. What time should I come over?" "How about six o'clock? Allie needs some company, too. She gets tired of listening to me," Ruth chuckled.

"What can I bring?"

"Not a thing, Mabel. I'll tend to it. See you after while."

"See you then, Ruth."

Ruth put the receiver back on the cradle and stared at the refrigerator. "Good idea. I need to get back to cooking, and Mabel will give me a reason to do it."

Ruth took a package of chicken from the freezer and placed it in the sink to thaw. Then, rather than disturb the now-sleeping Allie, she sat in the other recliner and began to read. She hardly got into her magazine article before she began to nod and then fell asleep.

The doorbell rang, Allie jumped from her chair and started for the front door, and Ruth awakened—all at what seemed the same instant for Ruth. She followed the dog and opened the door to accept a small arrangement of cut flowers from a delivery boy. Back in the kitchen, she placed the arrangement on the counter, opened the card, and read it out loud: "Just thinking about you. Love, Kevin and Sandra."

Ruth flashes a sad smile and tells Allie, "I never thought Dad and I had so many friends. What wonderful neighbors." She picked up the telephone and dialed quickly from memory. But after glancing at the clock, Ruth put the phone down and said, "Lost track of the time. Mlle. They won't be home from work for a while yet. I'll call them later. Let's go for a walk."

* * *

Four days later, Ruth hurried through her breakfast routine, forgetting all about the newspaper on the front porch, obviously preoccupied and saying very little to Allie until she decided.

"Come on Allie. We're going to try something."

Ruth put on her coat and gloves and then went to the desk and took out the car keys. Excited by the jingle of the keys, Allie pranced in circles and headed for the door to the garage, Ruth right behind her.

"I may get myself into deep trouble, Allie, but I'll never know until I try."

Ruth opened the car door. Allie jumped in and bounded across to the passenger side as Ruth pushed the button on the wall of the garage. As the door bounced open, she eased into the driver's seat of the car.

"I was watching Mabel yesterday on the way to and from church, and I think I've got this down pat. Key in the ignition, turn, and don't hang on too long."

The car started and ran quietly.

"Let's see, Allie. I can't quite reach the pedals. How do you get this seat to come up? Here it is. Let's try this."

Ruth pulled the handle on the side of the seat; the seat slid backward. She tried again, this time holding the steering wheel with one hand and pulling forward as she pulled on the little handle with the other hand. The seat moved too far forward, and she nervously pulled and pushed until it felt right. Her hands shook, and she began to cry. She found a tissue in her coat pocket, wiped her eyes, and leaned forward until her forehead touched the steering wheel. She sat motionless until Allie nuzzled her arm.

"I've got to stop this. Allie. I can't do anything while I'm crying."

She stuffed the tissue back into her pocket and looked over the dials and knobs that she had never paid much attention to before yesterday. She fastened her seat belt.

"The mirror. I need to fix the mirror so I can see what's back of me. Now, I want to back up. That's the '**W**.'"

Ruth held her foot tightly on the brake pedal and squeezed the button on the gearshift lever like Mabel had done. She then pulled it downward to the letter 'JR'. With the car in reverse, pushing hard on the brake, Ruth sat still for several seconds. The car remained motionless.

"Here goes nothing, Allie. Hold on. I'll ease up on this pedal and see what happens."

The car began to move very slowly, and Ruth immediately pushed hard on the brake pedal. Her body was tense, and little beads of perspiration dotted her forehead, even though the temperature was near freezing outside. Allie barked excitedly.

"Hold your horses, Allie. I don't want to get us hurt. I'll try this again and see if we can move out of the garage. Easy does it!"

Ruth lifted her foot off the brake and felt the car move backwards, ever so slowly. Then she realized that she needed to know where the car was going. She looked into the rearview mirror, but while looking at the open space behind her, she forgot the brake pedal and let her foot move completely off, causing the car to move more rapidly. Panicked, Ruth jerked the steering wheel to the left. The passenger side of the car careened into the garage door frame at the same instant Ruth remembered to push on the brake pedal.

"Oh no, Allie! Look what I've done!"

Not understanding the seriousness of the situation, Allie barked her own excitement.

"Now what do I do? I've got to get out of here! What kind of damage have I done? What is Will going to say? Be calm, Ruth. I can't just leave the car running. How does Mabel shut everything down? I'll just turn off the key, that's what. Wait, this thing must go to the `P'."

Still shaking, Ruth fumbled with the door handle, opened the car door, and got out to survey the damage. She walked to the passenger side and saw a badly bent fender and some splintered wood around the garage door frame. She began to cry and then eased her body down the side of the car until she collapsed on the floor of the garage. Allie jumped from the open driver's side door, ran around the car, and nudged Ruth's arm. With one hand, Ruth hugged the dog; with the other, she continued to wipe her eyes. They sat still for several minutes as though neither was sure what to do next.

Finally, Ruth shoved the tissue into her pocket, got up somewhat stiffly, and said, "Come on Allie. I'm not the first person ever to bump into something. Get back in the car, and we'll see if we can get it back in place. We can't just leave it here. What would the neighbors think?"

She started the engine again and ran through her memorized directions. Her eyes moved from instruments to lever to pedals. Finally, she pushed the brake pedal and pulled the gearshift lever to "D." Holding her breath, she eased the car forward inch by inch until it cleared the damaged door frame. When the car seemed headed slightly toward the other wall, she corrected the direction with the steering wheel and eased the car into its original position. When Ruth was certain everything was lined up properly, she tried to turn off the motor, but she discovered she needed to put the car in park. Then she turned off the motor. Only then did she breathe easy again.

"Come on, Allie. Let's look this thing over."

Ruth walked around to the passenger side of the car and ran her hand over the bent area.

"Not too bad! I think it'll still drive, though it's not too pretty. Let's see that garage door frame. Hmm.... Not pretty either, but I think it might still work."

Allie barked encouragingly. Ruth slid her hand along the door track. "Let's see if this'll still work, Allie."

She walked over to the button on the wall and pushed it, keeping her hand on the button just in case she needed to stop the door part way down. The door bounced downward, hesitating a bit but not stopping until it reached the bottom.

"Lucky. We're mighty lucky, Allie. Now what are we to do about all this? Well, you've had your ride. Brave dog. Probably cured us both of cars. Let's go inside and think about this."

Ruth went into the house with Allie close behind, neither of them quite sure what had just happened. Ruth sat in the recliner, and Allie sat close to her feet.

"Allie, this is a mess. I can get the car repaired, but how in the world could I get it to the dealer? Even if I could drive it there—and today proved to us both that I can't—I'd have to get Mabel to bring me home, and I'm not going to tell her what I've done. And I refuse to let Will know about this. He has too much to do anyhow. I'm just not going to tell him."

The dog sat motionless, looking up as though she understood. Ruth gave her a pat on the head and got up to go to the closet to hang up her coat and put away her gloves.

"I'll tell you what, Allie. I wrecked the car, but I got it going, and we didn't hurt anybody. I don't plan to give in just yet. Give me a couple of days to get rid of the shakes, and we're going to try it again. Yes Ma'am! I know I can at least back that car in a straight line—if I don't get distracted! That won't get us too far, but it'll be an improvement on today. If you're not afraid to go with me, we'll try it again."

Allie wagged her tail and danced in a circle, barking with excitement.

* * *

"This is the big day, Allie! I've backed that car out the driveway to the street three days in a row, and I got it back into the garage each time without hitting anything. Now we'll see if we can take it around the block."

Ruth put on her coat and gloves, took the keys from the desk, and stopped at the door to pat Allie on the head. They hurried through the den door and down the steps to the garage together. Allie barked and wagged her tail as Ruth pushed the garage door button. As the door moved up the track, Ruth opened the car door and Allie bounded into her seat. Ruth started the car with the confidence acquired from her practice tries and went through her mental list. Key in the ignition, foot on the brake, gear shift to 'It', ease off the brake, and the car moves backward inch by inch until it reaches the end of the driveway and the beginning of the street.

"Better close that garage door, Allie."

Ruth took the remote control in hand, found the button, pointed it as though it might explode, and pressed the button. The door crawled downward, and Ruth replaced the control on the dashboard.

"Now, Allie, let's see which way I have to turn this wheel."

The car rolled backward out of the garage, and Ruth turned the wheel too sharply and too quickly, running the car over the corner of the lawn and perilously close to a bush. She put the car in drive and inched it forward until it was back on the driveway. She tried to back out again, this time successfully.

"Now, Allie, we're ready. I'll just turn this wheel and go real slow until we get it straightened out."

Finally, on the street and headed in the right direction, the speedometer barely registered movement, but Ruth steered the car straight. At the corner, she stopped for the stop sign.

"It's a good thing most of the neighbors are at work, Me. Almost no traffic. The good Lord takes care of fools and little children. Let's go right. Four right turns, and we'll be back at home."

The car inched around the corner and toward the next stop sign, and to the next, and then the next. The entire journey was completely uneventful, except for the speed of the car, which was interminably slow since Ruth never removed her foot completely from the brake pedal. Back at her driveway, she made her final turn and guided the car into the garage. She returned the gearshift to "P," turned off the motor, and looked at Allie.

"Ha! How do you like that, my friend? I just drove this thing all the way around the block. You knew I could do it all the time, didn't you?!"

Allie barked her agreement and nuzzled her head against Ruth's arm. They remained in the car for several minutes, Ruth smiling and Allie leaning against her arm.

***

"Allie, we've been around the block five days in a row without any trouble, and we got through two visits with Will without him seeing that damage to the car. I've got something to attend to today."

Allie barked, and Ruth picked up the telephone book, looked up a number, and dialed.

"Hello, I'd like to speak with Ray."

After a few moments, Ray was on the phone.

"Ray, this is Ruth Johnson. I've got a problem with the car, and I need some help."

"I'm glad to help you any way I can, Ruth. What's the problem?"

"The car has a dented front fender. It's bothering me to see it. I wonder if you could have one of your people come get the car, fix it for me, and then bring it back?"

"Sure, Ruth, what happened to the car?"

"Well, if you don't mind, I'd rather not talk about how it happened. I just want it put back like it was when it was new."

"No problem. I'll send Jim around to your house around noon today to pick up the car, if that's convenient for you."

"Thank you, Ray. I'll see you at church on Sunday. Bye-bye."

As Ruth hung up the telephone, Allie ran to the pantry and returned with her leash.

"No, Allie. We can't go anywhere until Jim comes for the car. Then I'm going somewhere, but we'll go for a walk when I get back."

Ruth and Allie ate lunch, interrupted by Jim's arrival to pick up the car. Ruth cleaned up the table quickly and again looked for a number in the phone book. She called for a taxi.

"Allie, I'm going to the DMV to get one of those driver's books. I called them and found out that if I want to get a license, I have to take a test. They told me about this manual. While we wait for the car to be fixed, I'll study that book and get the permit you have to have to learn to drive. Can you beat that? I already know how to drive, and I still have to get a permit! If that's what you have to do, that's what I'll do. 'Jumping through hoops' is what Dad called it. Everybody has to do it. I just hope this works. I haven't taken any kind of test in years."

Allie barked encouragingly.

* * *

One week later, the car, repaired and newly washed, sat in the garage. Ruth and Allie sat in the den. They were both filled with excitement; Ruth because of her own victory and Allie happy because Ruth was happy.

"I only missed one question, Allie. Just one! And the clerk said my eyes were fine to drive, as long I have my glasses on. Well, I always have my glasses on. I didn't run the car into the side of the garage because I didn't see it; I ran into the wall because I didn't know what I was doing, and I got scared. But I know now, and I don't intend to run into anything else. Tomorrow, we're going to go for another ride, and every day after that until I think I've got this driving thing down just right."

Allie barked and jumped into Ruth's lap to nuzzle her face. Ruth hugged Allie and began to cry.

"I wonder if Dad would be proud of me. I wonder if I ought to be upset with him for not helping me to do these things a long time ago. Oh, what does it matter? I just miss him.

* * *

"Let's see, Allie. I've called Mabel and Kevin and Sandra. I don't think anybody else would be worried if they were to call tonight and we weren't here."

Allie barked in agreement.

"I'll leave a couple of lights on and the radio playing. I've got a few things in the suitcase, just what I'll need for one night. This is the first time I've spend a night away from home since Dad died. In fact, I don't remember ever spending a night away from this house without Dad."

Ruth knelt to hug Allie, wiped her eyes with the back of her hand, and stood up.

"Let's see how we do, Allie."

Ruth and Allie followed what had become a ritual: they went out the door and down the two steps into the garage; up went the garage door; they got in the car, Allie first and Ruth right behind her. Ruth started the car and eased it out of the garage, stopped the car long enough to close the garage door, and continued toward the street; and there, she backed out, put the car in drive, and pulled slowly away from the house.

"When we get to the DMV, Allie, you get on the floor of the back seat, and don't move a muscle," Ruth warned cheerfully. "That officer might not want a dog in the car while I'm taking that driving test."

Ruth drove carefully on the route she had rehearsed again and again, pausing with each change of direction to recite aloud the rules she memorized.

"Full stop. Look both ways. Turn signal. Check rear view mirror. Turn. Turn signal. Check side mirror. Change lanes. Turn signal off. Turn signal right. Turn. Full stop."

After a few more turn signals, turns, and stops, Ruth arrived in the DMV parking lot, where she stopped and turned off the ignition.

"All right, Allie. Back seat. No noise, okay? I'll be right back."

"Thank you for your help, officer. All I do is take this paper inside and they give me my license? Just like that?"

"Yes, Ma'am, that's it," the officer said.

Ruth smiled like a sixteen-year-old.

"Thank you very much!" she said.

As the officer walked away from the car, Allie barked and jumped

into the front seat. The officer turned in surprise, and shaking his head with a grin, he walked toward the next applicant. Ruth disappeared into the DMV building and returned several minutes later holding her purse and a little plastic card. All smiles, she got back into the car, but this time she turned in a different direction upon leaving the parking lot. They were not headed towards home.

"We're on a run of luck, Allie. Let's find out if Will and Mary and Billy are up for a couple of surprise house guests!"

DORA

"You must be Reverend Andrews. Good evening. I'm Lettie, Ted's wife. Please come in."

Landon Andrews stepped inside the door as he shook Lettie's extended hand.

"Please call me Landon. I'm sorry I wasn't here yesterday, but I was out of town and just heard about Dora's death from the church secretary an hour ago. I'm not even sure what happened."

Lettie didn't seem to have heard the last part of Landon's reply. She answered, "Thank you for being here now. Ted is in the den on the phone with someone from the hospital. Before I tell him you're here, could I have a word with you in the living room?"

Landon nodded and they left the hallway and went to the matching pair of facing love seat sofas and sat opposite each other.

"Ted loved his mother as much as it's possible to love anyone," she began. "Since yesterday, he has gone from heavy tears to stoic acceptance to business with the telephone and paper shuffling, all in a matter of a few hours. I wonder if we could ask you to go with us to the funeral home tomorrow. Frankly, the thought of going there is so frightening to both of us. And neither one of us is thinking clearly."

Landon smiled sympathetically. "Of course, I will if that's what you want. I usually offer to meet the family at the funeral home so I can be a resource in planning the service."

"What a relief," Lettie replied. "I'll go and see if Ted's off the phone. Is that the doorbell again? Please make yourself at home." The words trailed off behind her as she hurried to the front door.

Landon stood up to stretch, looked around the room, and simply followed his eyes as he walked from area to area. He paused in front of the walnut

bookcase, on which sat a photograph of Dora and her husband Burl. "Olan Mills." Probably one of those church directory pictures. Dora's expression seemed firm but warm. Burl? What was that look? Like he was far away. Chest reluctantly tucked behind Dora's shoulder, as though he didn't want to be there, in the picture, in that room, anywhere. Dora had told Landon that the family physician suspected the beginnings of Alzheimer's disease. Some agitation and erratic behavior a couple weeks ago had caused the family and the doctor to admit Burl to the state psychiatric hospital for evaluation. Landon thought it strange that no one had mentioned Burl in all this turmoil. He was, after all, Dora's husband.

Landon had come to St. Mark's Church only three months earlier. A small town of about fifteen thousand people, Williston rapidly was becoming a bedroom community for Louisville, Kentucky. St. Mark's consisted of a few more than three hundred households, but many of those families claimed only a marrying-burying relationship with the church. In three months, he had hardly gotten a good start on learning names, much less the histories and relationships of the people.

He knew Dora, however. Everyone knew Dora. When Landon and his family arrived, Dora was one of the first to appear at their door and even brought a hot peach pie to welcome them. Landon needed little time to assess Dora's spiritual depth and dogged determination. She could be loving and affirming, but she had little hesitation about being confrontational when she thought she needed to be. She spoke her mind and ruffled some feathers, but she got away with it because she was almost always right. Landon had thought several times that if Dora had been born fifty years later, she might have become a corporate executive.

The doorbell rang again and Landon heard Lettie scurry to answer it. The caller must have handed her a dish of food and left. Lettie returned to the kitchen just as Ted entered the living room. He greeted his mother's priest with a sad smile, droopy shoulders, and weary eyes. The two men shook hands.

"Reverend Andrews, I can't thank you enough for coming," Ted said. "I'm just so confused and upset. And I apologize for keeping you. If I don't make a call, someone else calls here. It's almost too much to deal with. I'd like to get out of this house and away from people for a few minutes. Oh, but I don't mean you of course. Mother thinks—I mean thought—so much of you."

The minister smiled warmly and asked Ted to call him by his first name. "Well, Landon, then. Mother said you like to walk. Would you mind if we just went outside for a while? I need to get out of this house."

"Certainly," Landon answered as Lettie returned to the living room.

"Lettie, would you mind if Landon and I went for a walk?" Ted asked. "Not at all," she replied. "In fact, I think it would help."

The two men went out the kitchen door and started down what appeared to be a very old wagon road. The autumn evening had begun to settle over the colorful trees and gently rolling hillside to the west. As they walked, Ted set a brisk pace, both with his feet and with his words.

"Mother bought this old farm over Dad's objection," Ted began. "That's kind of how things were done. Mother made the decisions. But I think it worked out. They got it for a very good price because the house was so run down. She knew Dad could fix anything, and he did. But it always had to be what she wanted fixed and the way she wanted it done. I think sometimes about how hard it must have been for Dad. She was always right! But I think he did what she wanted because he loved her so much. Funny how two people who care for each other so deeply can disagree so sharply.

"That little shop there by the barn. Dad built it, I think so that he could have some place to himself. I loved to spend time with him there, with the smell of sawdust and the sound of the tools and the magic of all those things hanging on the walls. In the winter, he kept a wood stove burning."

They walked past the workshop and on toward the barn and took a clear path down a ravine. Ted spotted an old fallen tree and sat down. Landon was glad for the rest; Ted had been walking and talking at an almost breakneck speed.

"He did such a good job on the house. Lettie and I love it. Damn, it feels good to be away from all those phone call and visitors. But where was I? Oh, yes. Lettie and I graduated from college and married; a few years later, Mother announced that she and Dad—of course actually she—had bought a little house in town and 'they' wanted to know if we would like to live on the farm. Lettie was deliriously happy. I must admit that, as much as Mother controlled her own house, she has never interfered in our lives. And she and Lettie got along well. So we moved out here."

Ted jumped up and started on down the ravine talking as he went. Landon moved with him in silence.

"Mother retired three years ago, and I didn't like what I saw, but I guess I denied it. Dad didn't have his days to himself anymore; instead, he had Mother at home all day every day, except when he could sneak out here to spend time in his workshop. There was a lot of tension between the two of them. That triggered Mother's talk with Dr. Sams about some potential mental health issues with Dad. Landon, I really don't want to go back, but it is beginning to get dark."

Landon was relieved. Ted's walking pace was proving to be a challenge even though the priest considered himself to be in fairly good shape. As they made their way back up the ravine, Landon decided to take a risk and ask Ted about his father.

"Ted, I'm planning to go by the hospital to see your Dad when I leave here. Would you like to go with me?"

Ted stopped and leaned on an old hickory tree.

"The doctor asked me not to come tonight," Ted said. "Dad had been in the hospital for two weeks and they had just determined that he was well enough to spend the weekend at home. I think the doctors wanted to see how well he would do if he was discharged completely. He had just been home yesterday morning for a couple of hours when ...." Ted's voice trailed off as he stifled a sob.

Landon did not know Burl had come home. This story was taking an alarming turn. Landon hadn't pressed for the details of Dora's death, but now he needed to know the truth. He gently asked Ted what had happened.

"You don't know?" Ted looked shocked and then confused, but he continued. "Yesterday, one of the neighbors saw Dad sitting on the porch steps with his hands cupped around his face. She went over to him and noticed that he was crying. She asked him what was wrong, and he pointed to the house. She went to the door, saw Mother on the floor, and called 911. The ambulance came. Dad was all to pieces, sobbing, incoherent. The police called Dr. Sams and then immediately took him back to the hospital. Of course, they will want me to see him, but the doctor asked me to give them tonight to calm him down and I agreed. I think they have him heavily sedated."

Ted pushed himself away from the tree and resumed his walking, but now his gait was slow and pensive. The men walked in silence for several minutes. Landon tried to process this surreal scenario and his own overwhelmed emotions. He thought about what lay ahead, the funeral with a huge number of people, grief work with Ted, Lettie and Burl, and many people in the church and town. He felt terribly inadequate.

The men came to edge of the yard and near the neat little wood-frame workshop. A cleverly carved wood sign graced the lintel above the double entry doors. It read, "BURL'S PLACE." Ted paused. "Let's go in," he said.

"Sure," responded Landon. He was curious. Ted opened one of the doors, entered the shop and switched on an overhead shop light.

The inside was so neat it hardly looked like a real workshop. Every tool appeared to be in its own specifically designated place. The power machinery was all wiped clean. The gable roof was exposed and the rafters provided storage for hundreds of feet of lumber, pieces of metal, pipes, and other building materials. All of it had been placed arranged in precise order.

As he looked around his father's workshop, Ted's eyes misted over and then the tears furrowed gently down his cheeks and onto his chest. He took out a handkerchief and wiped his face. He then took a shop rag and wiped off two rustic split log benches, each designed for one person. They sat in silence until Landon happened to notice that daylight had all but gone. Ted broke the silence.

He shook his head as he said, "We may never understand why Dad shot her."

IRENE

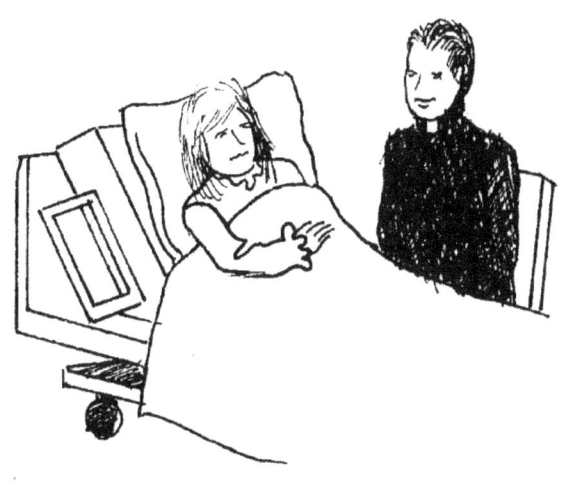

Preston's pace was brisk, his heels clicking on the ceramic floor of the hospital corridor announcing his approach well in advance of his actual entrance. He entered the room and smiled cheerily to the patient in the first bed and nodded a silent but pleasant greeting to the other elderly lady in the bed next to the window. His smile was usually warm and his body full of energy. It was Friday, however, and Preston was feeling somewhat drained.

Nevertheless, he was determined not to let his weariness show. Once this visit was over, he could go home and relax. He pulled a straight chair to a spot between the first bed and the wall so he could face the patient and offer his undivided attention. But his attention was divided. His mind was spinning with all sorts of responses to a frustrating day and an overflowing week.

Irene reached out her hand and smiled broadly. She was obviously delighted to see him.

"I knew that was you when I heard those footsteps. I can always tell your walk!"

In one motion, he took her hand, patted it kindly, seated himself, and asked out of habit, "How are you today?"

As soon as the words left his mouth, Preston knew he was in for it. Such a question for Irene was carte blanche for a description of every detail of the day. She hardly paused for an uneasy breath, frequently adjusting the green oxygen tube resting on her ears and just under her nasal passages. She droned on and on about two "spells" earlier that day. He knew those to be partially the result of fatigue from the simplest of tasks; it could have been bathing, having her bed changed, or eating her meals. Even sitting up in the chair on the other side of her bed could trigger the attacks. He also knew that this shortness of breath frightened her so much that it became harder still for her to breathe. Each time Irene became exhausted, breathing became more difficult, fear set in, and a spiral of crises followed. Slightly labored breathing, fear of another "spell," tenseness of body, struggle for breath more pronounced, fear turned up a notch, gasping for breath, panic, nurses summoned, several minutes of efforts to calm her down and to increase her oxygen intake, and the rest of the day in utter weakness.

Preston knew it must be distressing, but he had heard this all before.

During Irene's medical monologue, Preston listened, nodded, frowned, interjected an occasional "Really?" and sympathized with an "Oh no!" several times. He hoped she would remain calm and not work herself into another spell, since the spells could also be brought on by non-stop talking. Even though she herself knew this, Irene continued her account without so much as a period at the end of any sentence or even a pause to indicate a change in thought. Preston suspected she did this because if she hesitated he might have the chance to look at the time, stand up, and say goodbye. Irene didn't have many visitors and she wasn't eager to let one go.

Irene had been retired from the telephone company for more than a decade. She lived alone until lung surgery two years earlier. Her only family consisted of a nephew who lived across the street and a niece in a nearby city. She had several friends from her women's club; they were all close to her age and either widowed, divorced, or had never married. They met monthly, got together between meetings, and chatted on the telephone almost daily. They were also an arts and crafts group, which provided handmade table favors for local banquets, nursing home meal trays, and church functions. The group stayed busy and they enjoyed one another's company.

As long as Irene had been well, she filled her days with activities, and her loneliness was less pronounced. She crocheted tiny Christmas wreaths and made papier-mâché angels, attended her meetings, and went to lunch with "the girls." The lab report had been like an explosion to her; the surgery was difficult, and her recovery was extremely slow. The physical weakness that followed, as well as the fear of the disease she refused to pronounce, seemed to uncover an aloneness she had never allowed herself to admit.

Preston listened as attentively as he could, but he was increasingly conscious of the hardness of the wood-bottomed chair. His legs felt cramped by the narrow space they occupied. His stomach felt tight, and his shoulders ached. He thought about Irene's loneliness, her need to have someone listen, and the therapeutic value of community, even if that community consisted only of himself and Irene. But Preston also found himself glancing out the window at the September wind stirring the still-green Virginia woods. This was his last obligation for the day and it came later in the afternoon than usual. He was tired and wanted some time for himself. He found himself resenting Irene's non-stop litany of apprehensions, her "organ recital" of aches and pains. He felt irritated with himself for sitting down; if he had remained standing, he could have controlled the time a bit better. Most of all, he knew he had set himself up by asking, "How are you?" To ask a lonely and fearful person such a question was to invite an interminable answer.

Nevertheless, Preston listened out of professional habit, only half-conscious of Irene's flow of words.

"I can't make up my mind about that heart test Dr. Maxon wants me to have. Everybody tells me it's my own decision, but I think it might be dangerous to have that tube put all the way from my groin to my heart. But if it will help me to breathe better and get me back on my feet, it might be worth it. Dr. Maxon wouldn't ask me to do anything that isn't the best for me, would he? So, I talked to George Sutter's wife, and she said he had it done. After that, he had a big operation and now he feels better than he has in years."

Irene paused, not because she had no more to say, but because she was almost breathless. Preston had a feeling he knew what was on her mind: "If I stop talking, he will excuse himself and leave, and I'll be alone again." But as tired as he was, Preston fought off the temptation to do just what Irene feared.

He imagined Irene's day. Cleaning personnel, nursing staff, respiratory therapist, one or two physicians, her nephew—each person breezing into the room, talking to her while they performed some essential function or wrote on a chart, asking questions or making a comment without really paying attention to her, and then flitting from the room.

Even the nephew, who came by two or three times a week, only stayed for a few minutes. He did what he could, but he had a family of his own, a job, and only so much energy. For two years, he had tried to manage Irene's finances, her little cottage, and her personal needs. His sister had not been much help because of the distance between their homes.

Two years of illness had lengthened the time between visits from practically everyone in Irene's life. Her family and close friends were still involved, but with less frequency since the initial diagnosis and treatment. Irene was a people person. She loved to talk. As her crisis continued, she needed people more than ever, and she seemed to have them less than ever. Despite his weariness, Preston decided that he could not fail her. She needed him, and he wanted very much to provide her with the attention she wanted and deserved.

"Irene, I'm impressed with the way you seem to be working on this decision. You told me Wednesday that you had asked Dr. Maxon for a couple of days to think about the heart catheterization; you've obviously been thinking about it. You've also talked with your nephew and some friends. You recognize the risk and the possible benefits. It sounds to me like you're close to a decision." Preston paused, and Irene was waiting.

"Rev. Hollowell, if the doctors could just give me some guarantees, but of course that's not possible. I'm so afraid I'll make the wrong decision."

Her anxious and breathy voice labored on and on, and Preston felt a sharp pain in his arthritic knee. He was conscious of an involuntary grimace and hoped Irene didn't notice. Sometimes he felt like an old man, even though he was not quite fifty years of age. The pain reminded him of two boring meetings in his office earlier in the day. One had to do with church finances and the other involved a complaint from one of his staff. Both issues were recurring, common to most organizations, and frequent in churches.

Such problems were hardly the most rewarding aspects of parish ministry, as far as Preston was concerned, and he seldom allowed them to become irritants to him. But for whatever reasons, the two morning meetings had been for him anything but routine. Preston felt guilty for being bored and irritated by them; then he felt like a pious ass because he expected so much of himself. His sore knee reminded him again of the gap between his own lofty expectations of himself and limitations he'd rather ignore.

A slight increase in the volume of Irene's monologue brought him back into the room.

"I just keep thinking about the other operation, how much pain I went through, and how long it took me before I could go back to my house. And when I got home, it was months before I could do any of my work, cook my own meals, or go anywhere."

Irene paused, coughed, adjusted her oxygen tube, and tried to catch her breath. Preston shifted in his chair, rubbed his knee, nodded, and smiled to Irene as if to say, "Take your time; I'm not going anywhere."

Irene continued, "But you know, Rev. Hollowell, I never did get back to my old self. Gave my nephew's son my car. I couldn't drive it anymore, and he needed it, with his wife and their new baby, just trying to get started, and his daddy's been good to me."

Preston's mind went back to several visits in Irene's home, first when he had become minister of her church and later after her surgery. At the time of his first visit, Irene's house was a veritable clutter of materials for her crafts. Folding tables were filled with various paper cuttings, bangles, pipe cleaners, wires, scissors, paints, and on and on. The folding tables continued out of sight into other rooms, each one overflowing as the first. The furniture was almost unusable because of all the tiny dolls, decorated candleholders, clothespin figures, pillows, cloth, and paper. Unwashed dishes and cooking utensils overran the kitchen sink. Boxes of finished items were stacked near the front door, waiting to be delivered to some worthy affair the next day.

No visitor could have been confused about Irene's interests and priorities, or her devotion to what she loved.

Preston remembered her half-hearted apology for "this mess," and the thoroughly delightful lessons on how easy it was to make each item. He remembered Irene's apology for not having been in worship the previous Sunday: "I'm afraid I've just been busier than I should be with all these projects!" In the years to follow, Irene never got any less busy, nor did she ever attend worship. It took lung surgery to stop her "projects." In his visits to Irene's home following the surgery, Preston noticed that the clutter of her work remained, although to a lesser degree. She continued to attempt a few small jobs. Her niece had stayed with her for a few days; she had imposed some order on the place. Friends came in occasionally to do some straightening up. But when Preston visited her home after the surgery, their conversation about her crafts was limited. Irene's unbounded excitement had been substantially compromised. And her sense of being alone no longer had a hiding place in the clutter of her hobbies.

The part of these post-surgery visits Irene seemed to enjoy most was when Preston would pray for her. Each time, after a report from Irene about her health and some words of encouragement from Preston, he concluded his visit with a prayer. Preston never had to suggest this; Irene always sensed the moment and said, "You're going pray for me before you go, aren't you?" Each prayer ended with a hint of a tear in Irene's bright eyes.

Her "religion?" It certainly did not include public worship, as far as Preston could tell. She had never after that first visit offered further apology for not attending Sunday services. She expressed no regret during her illness for not being able to go to church, and she never in any way indicated that when, or if, she recovered she planned to attend. Yet, she welcomed and appreciated Preston's ministry. He suspected that Irene had initially been flattered that the minister of her church had come to see her; during her surgery, he surmised, she had welcomed him because of her fear, her pain, and her heightened awareness of death. Recently, he sensed that she had accepted him as a priest sent by God to assist her in her troubles.

Preston Hollowell knew what qualities he needed to be a good minister: depth of spirit and compassion. He wanted these attributes to be in his life all the time. But today, they were not there. He sat as still as possible. He listened as carefully as he could. He smiled as warmly as he should. He understood the essential nature of Irene's struggle. He had a good idea how important he was to her. But, right at that moment, he did not want to be there. He resented her non-stop talking. He felt some impatience with her struggle over the impending heart catheterization. And, most of all, Preston was irritated with himself for being tired, for having a sore knee, and for wanting to be home in his easy chair.

Irene continued, and Preston heard her talking about Dr. Maxon again.

"He's nice enough," she said, "but he's so busy. He comes in with all his papers, stands at the end of the bed, and asks me how I feel. He comes in every day, but he hasn't said anything about that test since Monday. I'd like to ask him some questions, but he never sits down."

Preston noticed that Irene had been speaking a little less rapidly, even pausing for breath, as if she trusted him not to leave if she paused.

"Let me make a suggestion," Preston interrupted. "When Dr. Maxon comes in, tell him that you have been thinking about the test he mentioned and you would like to talk to him about it and ask a few questions. Ask him if he could sit down and talk to you. I'm sure he will want to answer your questions, and he may be waiting for you to let him know you are ready to make a decision. After all, I think you told me that he said there was no hurry."

Irene nodded as though she liked the suggestion, and then she continued, "Do you think he'll be upset with me if I tell him I'm not sure yet? I mean, he wouldn't have brought it up if he didn't think I ought to do it. I can't make up my mind, and I'm pretty nervous about the whole thing because he said there was some risk involved. That means in doctor-talk that it's dangerous. I've talked to some people, and I've thought about it, and I trust his opinion and all. But nobody wants to tell me what to do. I appreciate that, you know, but ...."

Preston interrupted again.

"Irene, nobody wants to make the decision for you. You have been through a great deal in the last two years. Possible heart surgery is pretty frightening to all your friends because nobody wants to see you suffer. Neither does anyone want to see you lie here, short of breath and unable to do the things you want to do. Everybody knows the decision is not simple. But I want you to know that I think you have done an excellent job trying to work through all this. You have thought, discussed, and weighed the options. By the time you have your talk with Dr. Maxon, you will be ready to decide, and we will all support you in whatever you choose, and so will Dr. Maxon."

Irene smiled broadly, and said, "You make me feel better already, and I think I know what to do. I just needed to talk about it. I'm glad I've got you for my minister!"

Preston felt a bit hypocritical, but he smiled, took Irene's hand, and asked her with a smile, "Do you think we should pray about this?"

"I sure do," she replied.

Preston bowed his head, still holding her hand, and he prayed for Irene to find healing of body, mind, and spirit. He prayed for her to make her decision courageously.

Although he prayed enthusiastically in part because he knew his visit was almost over, he wondered between the words how God could pay any attention to such a divided spirit as his seemed to be today. He remembered the lady in the other bed, and he mentioned her in his prayer. He then concluded with the customary, "Amen."

When he looked up, Irene was crying.

"Will you hug me?" she pleaded.

Preston stood up and awkwardly moved close to her bed. The head of the hospital bed had been rolled up far so that Irene was practically sitting up in the bed. He put his arm behind her head and around her shoulders, and she leaned her head on his chest. For a long minute, she cried and he held her.

After what seemed to him a long time, he took her hand and sat back down in his chair. For the first time since he had entered the room his attention was riveted on Irene. He forgot everything else, including himself.

She reached for a tissue with her other hand and tried to dam up the torrent of tears.

"I feel all by myself, and it's hard to make decisions when you're alone. I haven't been able to really talk to anybody about this all week.

Everybody comes in, and nobody sits down. I know they can't tell me what to do, and I don't want them to, but I still feel alone and you make me feel better. Thank you for letting me talk!"

Preston realized that on Wednesday when she had first mentioned the heart catheterization, he had not been aware of how deeply afraid she was. Irene took the hand he had been holding and used both her hands to wipe away the tears. She had stopped crying.

"I'm all right now," she said with an embarrassed smile.

Preston stood and smiled. He said he was glad he was able to offer some encouragement and would be interested to hear about her conversation with the doctor. He told her he would visit her again on Monday.

Preston returned the chair to its original place in the room, told the lady in the other bed goodbye, and set out down the hospital corridor at his usual brisk pace. He was no longer conscious of his weariness, and, for the moment at least, he was free of what had bothered him, bored him, and worried him during the past twenty-four hours. He whistled a few bars of a Bach minuet he remembered his daughter playing on the violin. He greeted some familiar faces among the hospital staff on the way to the front door and headed for his car.

In the parking lot, he pulled off his coat and removed his collar. The sun had disappeared and the area was wrapped in twilight.

"Will you hug me?"

Preston Hollowell smiled to himself.

LIZZIE

Every year, Mom called and arranged a day for me to come to her house and help her with spring kitchen cleaning. Mom was my dad's mother, but almost everybody in the family called her Mom. A few called her Lizzie, but I thought that was a terrible way to shorten a beautiful name like Elizabeth.

It was the same routine every year. I went to her house after school on the pre-arranged Friday, spent the night, and on Saturday helped with the cleaning. We took the kitchen furniture to the side yard, placed each piece on a few sheets of newspaper, and painted it all white. Mom didn't bother to wash it all down with soap water to get the dried-up food and dirt off it. "A waste of time," she always said. "We'll just paint over it." And we did. I could swear it got heavier each year with so many coats of paint, not to mention the dried food and dirt.

A table and four chairs. No leaf in the table, and it didn't matter; the two ends of the table were permanently stuck together in the middle from all the layers of paint. We emptied the corner cabinet of all the utensils that were usually ready to fall out each time someone opened the door. And my favorite: the cupboard with the flour bin. When the weekly supply of groceries was delivered, Mom poured the ten-pound bag of flour right into the shiny bin so she could sift it out as she needed it. The cupboard had an upper part and a lower part, each filled with canned goods and utensils. Best of all, it had a metal shelf in the middle. It pulled out so she could stand there and mix up flour and the stuff she needed to "throw together" a cake or a tray of biscuits. She really did throw together whatever she made; she never measured anything. The cakes seldom achieved a uniform shape after she globbed on the frosting. But that was fine with me; it tasted great and I didn't care much about looks any way.

Back to the furniture painting. It never took us long because we didn't have to be careful. After all, what is careful when you paint right over dirt and dried food? While the paint dried, we cleaned out the icebox, which was really an electric refrigerator, but everybody called it the icebox. The icebox held two precious items, especially for a young boy. The first was a fruit drawer with an ample supply of Red Delicious apples. I can't smell one to this day without thinking about Mom. The other was a glass quart jar of drinking water. More than once a day I could count on a loud reprimand.

"You been drinkin' out this bottle again? I told you to use a glass." How did she know I didn't use a glass? I guess she saw the crumbs of whatever I had been eating settled in the bottom. None of us grandkids ever got away with anything with Mom.

After we finished painting, we washed the windows in the kitchen and scrubbed and waxed the floor. Finally, about dark, we hauled the furniture back into the kitchen, where it served its purpose for another year, and replaced the contents of the cabinet and cupboard.

I got no pay because Mom had no money. That was because she and Pop hated each other, or at least I think they did. He was a railroader, night shift, and never gave Mom a dime as far as I knew. But Mom was clever. For her church money and a few other necessities, she ordered more groceries than she needed and sold them to my aunt. They were delivered and Pop paid the bill. I don't think Pop ever figured out the system.

I guess I ought to say a word about Pop. He always awakened midmorning, swung his short legs over the side of the bed, put a Camel cigarette in a holder and lit it. He got up and walked barefoot to the refrigerator and got his insulin, filled a needle, and returned to the side of his bed. By that time the ash on the cigarette had grown to about three-quarters of an inch. He swabbed his thigh with alcohol on cotton, popped the needle into his leg like a dart thrower while the now inch-long ash dropped onto his bare leg. Not to worry. Another alcohol swab took care of that.

Then came his bath, flooding the little shot-gun house with the scent of Life Buoy soap. I'll not forget that smell either. Bath done, dressing completed, the side show began. "Tell the old woman to hurry up with my breakfast; I've got to get out of here!" Sometimes Mom started the barbed conversation. "Tell the old man to get in here and eat his breakfast or I'll throw it out!" I never doubted she would have, or that she would have enjoyed doing it. I don't know what they did when I wasn't there, because they were only talking to one another through me. I never bothered to relay the messages since they delivered them loudly enough for even the neighbors to hear. Neither did I understand for the longest time why they stayed together if they hated each other so much.

"Stubborn old woman," he often said. "That's the Cherokee in her." Mom was indeed stubborn. I don't know enough about Cherokees to believe that had any connection. I don't remember, however, that she ever changed her mind about anything. She had sharp, summary opinions about everything and everybody, mostly about everybody. She often used a particular story to better label her next-door neighbor a hypocrite. Once, the preacher came to see this neighbor, and as he was about to knock on the screen door, he heard Mom's neighbor chide her grandchildren, "You kids quiet down; I'm tryin' to study my damned Sunday School lesson." The minister, Mom said, turned and left without knocking.

Even as a little guy I remember lying in my bed at Mom's house, thinking about the incongruity of her life. She rode to church on the church bus, twice on Sunday for services and once on Wednesday evening to the mid-week prayer meeting. She spent her other evenings with her Bible, glasses pinching the end of her nose, sometimes for hours. She never talked about what she read, so I don't know how or if any of it struck her in particular ways. I knew the Bible pretty well myself. Something seemed terribly wrong with intense Bible reading and church-going on the one hand, and what seemed to me to be intense hatred for Pop on the other hand.

She might have been claiming her right to be angry. Pop was a notorious womanizer, poker player, and harsh disciplinarian of his five children. I was told he made my father get a job or move out when the Depression hit. Dad moved out, rode boxcars west, and worked wherever he could find a job. Mom said she didn't hear from him for several years. On another occasion, Pop was said to have put a dog brought home by one of the five kids into a gunny sack, taken it on his train to a distant place, and let it out to fend for itself or worse. With many more stories like that, Mom had plenty of reasons to be angry at Pop, but how could she reconcile the Bible teachings with her anger? How did she survive his cruelty? I'm not sure we'll ever know the answers.

I know Mom loved me, maybe even more than any of the other grandkids, because I spent so much time with her and because I always helped her around the house and yard. She never hugged me or said she loved me, but I always had a sense that she cared for me and simply enjoyed having me around. Sometimes we rode the church bus together and I often sat with her in church. So strange to me, to love one person so much and hate another with the same intensity.

And I think Pop loved me the best he knew how. He took me for school clothes the day before the start of kindergarten. I never wore the knickers he bought me; I always suspected they were the last pair in the whole world. The times had passed him by. Pop paid me to mow the grass and put in the coal from outside the gate into the bin in the basement. Now that I'm older, I wonder if he tried to make up in me what he had done so badly in raising his own children.

Everything changed one day. One morning after Mom fixed Pop's breakfast, packed his lunch and he left for work, she packed something for herself. She packed two old pasteboard suitcases with the things she wanted to keep, caught a city bus and went to live with my aunt. No advance warning or request for permission. She just showed up on my aunt's doorstep and announced she had come there to live. My aunt asked her if she wanted her to go home with her and get some more of her things, but she said she had all she needed.

From that day on, she lived with my aunt, and then with my parents for a long while, and then in a small private nursing home. As far as I could tell, she spoke very little and never raised her voice again. Maybe she spent all the shouting she had on Pop. He never asked her to come home; probably he never communicated with her in any way. She never looked back. When Pop died, almost a decade before her death, she went to the funeral, sat dispassionately, and never shed a tear as far as anyone knew.

When Mom died at age ninety-six, she left me the last quilt she pieced together. I asked a friend to finish it for me. Instead, in her wisdom, she loaned me a hoop and some needles, thread, and thimbles. I worked on it through a long summer and learned why people in the past quilted only in the winter. With the quilt draped over my legs, I felt like I lost many pounds of sweat every evening.

It was a summer of remembering. The smell of Life Buoy soap, Red Delicious apples, and Pop's Camel cigarettes. And yes, the paint drying on the kitchen furniture. I was able to recreate the interior house in my mind. Every piece of blue-collar furniture, the pictures on the wall, the little old RCA radio, and especially the house dresses Mom wore.

When she took these dresses out of service, she recycled them into quilts like the one I was working on. But my quilt was all wrong. Green and orange were not complimentary colors, in my opinion. Nevertheless, the quilt reminded me of some of the dresses Mom wore. The uneven stitching, caused by eyesight gradually lost to glaucoma, would have been an embarrassment to her if her vision had been good enough to see what she had done. Her two greatest pleasures, quilting and Bible reading, were taken from her as her eyesight failed. Mom had told me she only went to school four years, and then only when she was free from field chores. The Bible reading must have been a struggle for her, but she never let on. I don't know whatever happened to that old, badly worn Bible, but I still have the quilt, and that's enough. I don't use it any longer; it hangs on a quilt rack, handmade for me by a friend for this special use.

I often think about Mom and her contradictory life and about the humor of it all, and also I think about the sadness. Her quilt hangs in my bedroom. It's not the prettiest piece of handwork, but it reminds me of how much I loved Mom and how much she loved me, imperfections and all.

LOIS

The front door was open even though the autumn chill had descended. Walter wanted to smell hot browns baking. Hers were not the ordinary hot browns cooked in a large skillet; the ones Lois made had her personal touch. Three discolored ramekins, individual size. Dad had been long dead but she never baked them without one for herself and one each for Walter and his Dad. Turkey, vegetables, cheese, and a thin crust. Her version contained a spot of dry sherry.

"I'm home," he called out. Tired from the coast-to-coast flight, a bit late, but cheery just the same. He had always announced his arrival from school the same way.

He put down his bag, pressed his way into the kitchen, and took his tiny mother into his arms.

"You told me you would be here yesterday," she said. "I made the hot browns, but you didn't come. I was worried."

"Why didn't you call me?" Walter asked.

"Couldn't find your telephone number."

"Mom, I told you exactly when the plane would land today and how long it would take to get the rental and get here. I'm sorry you were worried, but I'm here now and hungry for my hot brown."

"Well, go and unpack your things, freshen up, and have a drink. I'll get dinner started."

Walter hadn't been back home for three years. He and Sandy were glad that his mother agreed travel was easier for her than for the two of them with all their business obligations. And she liked to fly. Walter simply sent her the ticket to Seattle and arranged ground transportation for her, and it all worked well.

But Walter had been warned of a problem in a phone call from his mother's banker, a fraternity brother from Walter's college. Lois had encountered money problems, and Ron suggested that Walter might want to come home for a review of them. Walter was completely caught off guard by the call. He had never imagined his mother with money problems. Minutes into his visit, he could tell the problem was far deeper than money.

Every corner of every room, every piece of furniture, and even the bed in his old bedroom—everything was covered with boxes and packages, many unopened. Ceramics, lamps, pictures, wall hangings, decorative pieces, new telephones, linens, and practically everything else imaginable filled up all available space. The place looked like a warehouse. Finding a place to sit or uncovering his bed seemed a daunting chore. He opened the closet to hang his clothing, but that too was filled with more stuff. In the background, the television carried the excited voices of two people touting the blessings of a computer. "Only thirty-five more at this price! Don't let this one get by you!" Sure enough, there sat two large computer boxes from an earlier promotion; both were unopened.

Walter went out to the front porch and called Sandy on his cell phone. Yes, he arrived safely and on time. No, things were not well, and perhaps they were worse than he had imagined.

"Sandy, she didn't remember our phone number and couldn't find it. She thought I was coming yesterday. And the house is a clutter of brand new merchandise that I suppose she has been buying from the Home Shopping Club. I'm afraid of what else I'll find.... Yes, she looks good and hasn't forgotten how to make hot browns. I can smell them now.... I dread my appointments tomorrow with Ron at the bank and with Dr. Bellamy.... I'll call again tomorrow night. I love you."

"Walter, come and eat," his mother called from the kitchen.

She had a difficult time finding space at the dining room table and a place to unload two chairs, but she managed and made no apology. Hot browns in individual ramekins, yeast rolls, fruit salad, and sweet tea. Her cooking was as good as ever. Walter ate slowly and in almost abject silence, but Lois seemed not to notice. The meal almost completed, Lois went to the kitchen for slices of apple pie, which she had made from apples from the trees in the back yard. Walter wondered how things could be so incongruent this wonderful meal and Lois's apparent normalcy on the one hand, and the massive clutter and forgetfulness on the other.

Walter decided not to bring up financial matters and all the stuff in the house until the next day. He and Lois spent the evening catching up on the goings-on in the neighborhood. The evening was pleasant, but Walter couldn't stop wondering what exactly was wrong with his mother. He went to bed but slept very little that night.

* * *

Lois had retired from the classroom thirteen years ago. She had won the teacher of the year award in her state and competed in the national competition. She taught English and drama. The drama part defined her; she was always on-stage, flamboyant in her dress and speech. The students loved her, as did the entire community.

No one was sure when Lois began to slip, but some conjectured that the death of her husband nine years ago provided a gentle nudge into depression and loneliness. She continued to care for her own yard, fruit trees, and berry bushes, but the neighbors saw her house deteriorate. The exterior needed paint, the roof looked like its days were numbered, and the gutters were in desperate need of cleaning. Walter lay in bed wondering how things could have gone downhill in such short a time and how he had missed it all each time she visited him and Sandy. Perhaps Ron could help him know more about what was going on. And he would talk with Dr. Bellamy tomorrow after office hours.

* * *

Walter woke up to the aroma of fresh coffee, biscuits, eggs, and bacon. Apparently, he had slept better than he thought.

"What are your plans for today?" Lois asked.

"Lunch with Ron, and then I thought you and I could take a drive so I can see my old stomping grounds. How would that be for you?"

Lois was enthusiastic about the idea of getting out of the house. Her car had been in the shop for a week following a minor wreck. Another big issue, Walter thought, as though he needed another.

Later, Walter pulled up to the bank, turned off the motor, and eased his forehead to the steering wheel. He didn't want to learn what he feared was ahead.

At the information desk he introduced himself.

"Walter Nedley to see Mr. Browning."

"Yes, he is expecting you. First door on the left."

Ron's door was open and Walter walked in, shook hands with his friend, and sank into an overstuffed leather chair.

"How about if we talk business first and then catch up on our own stuff over lunch?' asked Ron.

"Good enough. Tell me what I need to know but don't want to know."

"It's not good, Walter. About six months ago, your mother came in and asked me for a loan against her house. I knew that she and your Dad were comfortable, that they had no debts. I told her the loan would be no problem but that I would need a few days to set it up. We made her the loan, several thousand dollars that I assumed would be for a new car or maybe some house repairs. But last week, one of the loan officers came in to tell me that she had made no payments on the loan and that his calls to her went unanswered. We ran some checks on her credit status and her bank records with us. I was shocked by what we found."

Ron continued with bad news. "She had many credit cards, all maxed out, utility bills in arrears, and a long list of overdrafts. I saw her in the lobby a few days before I called you, took her into my office, and asked her what was going on. Walter, she didn't have a clue. I double-checked the canceled checks. Charitable contributions, television evangelists, political action committees of both parties, and television shopping channels. Walter, the total has run into the thousands. The bank directors are close to foreclosing on her house, but I'm not sure a foreclosure would recover all that is needed to draw her even. I know she has her teachers' retirement, a small Social Security income, and your father's annuity. She could be all right if someone managed her money, but she isn't going to be able to live as comfortably as she used to."

"This is much worse than I expected," sighed Walter. "You should see the house. It's like a Home Shopping Club warehouse. And who knows what's in all those papers in the desk? Ron, Sandy and I could give her some money, but what would keep this from happening again?"

"Walter, I know this is a lot for you to take in. You've got some big decisions to make, but I'll help you any way I can."

Walter stared out the window for a moment and then stood up. "Let's go for some crab cakes, Ron. Seattle seafood is wonderful, but it could never match Maryland crab cakes. I'd like to hear about what's new with your family."

After lunch, Walter drove back to the house, but his mother had forgotten that they were going for a drive, so he waited in the car for her to change. When they got underway with the rented convertible's top down, Lois laughed as the wind blew her hair. In an instant, she looked twenty years younger. They drove from place to place, seeing their church, the old school, the new shopping center, and the yards Walter had mowed during high school. They talked about people who had gotten married, had children, died, or moved away and how dear the community had been to both of them.

The drive ended too quickly for Lois, but Walter had to drop her off at home so he could meet Dr. Bellamy at his office. The doctor's office was a mass of charts, books, samples of medicine not yet placed in the cabinets, and boxes of who knew what. Walter and Dr. Bellamy sat opposite each other in matching red leather chairs.

"Walter, because of federal regulations, I can't talk with you about your mother's health without a signed consent form, and I don't think that would be such a good idea to pursue that right now. I can, however, talk with you about aging, dementia, memory loss, and the pressure all these lay on families, but only in a general way. And I can listen to what you can tell me about what's going on at home."

"I understand," said Walter. "I'll try to fill you in on what I know and let you take it from there." Walter talked about the dent in his mother's car, apparently from some minor accident, her memory problems, her money problems, the clutter of boxes and packages in every room, and the general neglect of the house.

"Walter, I went through much of what you're describing with my own mother five years ago. When I was in med school, we were given a simple rubric to help evaluate elderly people. IMAJO: intellectual function, memory, affect, judgment, and orientation to time, place, and people. It was purely academic to me until I started practicing. I've seen it again and again. I saw it with my mother. She had written dozens of checks to charities, wrecked her car, melted down a couple of teapots, and would forget just about everything. Once we understood the extent of her problems, we had to take her car away, but aside from the occasional question about where she must have parked it, she didn't seem to notice. We moved her to a nice assisted living community, but she continued to deteriorate until she died. Near the end, she didn't recognize any of us. I felt powerless, both as a son and as a physician. Walter, you and Sandy have some decisions to make and probably not a lot of time in which to make them. Short of a miracle, people suffering from dementia just get worse and worse, but she may nevertheless have several good years left in the right environment."

Walter asked a few more questions and thanked Dr. Bellamy for his time. He tried to process all that he had learned today while driving back to his mother's house. He needed to talk with Sandy to get her input, for whatever solution he chose would certainly affect his wife too.

When he reached the house, Walter found that his mother had changed into a pretty red dress but couldn't remember why. Walter reminded her that he was taking her out for dinner. They enjoyed the meal at a table with a water view. Not wanting to spoil the evening with talk of financial and medical problems, Walter made small talk.

Back home, Walter decided to broach the subject with his mother. He hadn't talked with Sandy yet but wanted to test the waters to see how his mother would react to the news of her financial problems.

"Mom, I talked with Ron at the bank today about your money situation, and there are some problems. He told me about the house loan, the credit card bills, and the depleted savings account."

"What on earth are you talking about, Walter? You know your father left me very comfortable. Nothing has changed."

Walter looked around the dining room. There barely a place the eye could rest that wasn't stacked with her unopened home shopping purchases. Was that a pinball machine? He didn't know what to say. Clearly upset, Lois said goodnight and went to bed early. Walter sat at her desk and began to search through her papers. Many letters from the bank, the credit card companies, and other creditors were unopened. He organized them as best he could, wanting and not wanting to know exactly how bad things were, and called Sandy before he went to bed.

* * *

The next morning, Walter again was wakened by the smell of breakfast cooking. He quickly showered and shaved and made his way to the kitchen, a little worried that his mother's irritation from the night before might have carried over into the new day. Walter realized that he simply didn't know what to expect any more when it came to his mother's behavior. He was a bit relieved to realize that she didn't remember anything about the conversation that had upset her the night before.

Breakfast finished, Walter placed a small pile of the papers he had gone through the night before in front of his mother. He began to explain slowly and simply each bill and the facts that couldn't be denied.

"Walter, I don't understand any of this," Lois said, sounding like a confused little girl. They sat quietly for what seemed like an eternity to Walter. Finally, he broke the silence.

"Mom, Ron told me the bank has begun proceedings to foreclose on the house. We can't avoid this. We can only hope the sale brings enough money to cover your bills."

Lois sat in stunned silence until Walter suggested they go for a drive.

* * *

Two days later, Sandy arrived. She packed Lois's clothes, some personal items, and a few pieces of furniture and arranged to have them shipped to Seattle. Walter found a consignment shop that would take all of his mother's unopened purchases and mail a check when they were sold. Sandy called to have the utilities disconnected and filled out a change of address form at the post office. She called Lois's closest friends, her church, and a few neighbors.

Exactly one week after Walter arrived, the three of them stood outside the house. A single tear rolled down Walter's face, but his mother stood expressionless. He and Sandy couldn't figure out how much she understood about what was going to happen. He wondered if perhaps it was better if it passed like an arrow over her head without coming close to her heart.

They loaded their bags into the trunk of the car and climbed in. Walter sat in the back seat and Sandy drove. Before they left, Sandy put the car's top up. They were off to Seattle. No one said a word.

MARIAN

I always loved that house. The Cape Cod was really much larger than it appeared from the outside, although it seemed to get smaller to me as the years went by. I spent many summer weeks there and some weekends during the school year. College Park was a two-hour train ride from the town where I grew up, so it was an easy trip. I loved the college town, quiet and safe, with all kinds of places to explore on the bike Dad kept there for me.

The house was nestled on a cul-de-sac with many trees. There were two guest rooms and a bathroom on the upper floor. I considered one of those rooms my own. Aunt Marian's bedroom, the one she and Uncle Lewis had shared before he died, was on the main floor. The kitchen always seemed to smell of pies and cakes. She kept it so neat and clean, but then everything else in the house was the same way.

The living room welcomed guests but was never used otherwise. The furnishings were Philadelphia Federal period, eighteenth century neo-classic, all fine reproductions. The dining room was used only on formal occasions or for larger family gatherings. Its beautiful furnishings followed the eighteenth-century theme, including a hunt board and two corner cabinets with lovely Waterford crystal and fine china.

My two favorite rooms were Uncle Lewis's library and the breakfast nook. The library was a man's room. It smelled of cigars and had a well-worn leather sofa and chairs and a fireplace. A large painting of a fox hunt hung above the mantle. With its intricate pattern of reds and greens and blues, an equally-worn oriental rug completed the room.

Like the library, the breakfast nook was unlike anything in the rest of the house. It had a bright white table and chairs, a small cabinet a serving cart, and a window seat. The large bay window flooded the room with light. I often watched the birds outside from the padded window seat.

Uncle Lewis had been a very successful merchant in Chicago. After he sold the business and retired, he and Aunt Marian moved south for the slower pace, the warmer weather, and all the cultural amenities of a college town. They blended in quickly, according to my dad. I don't remember anything about the move since I was still in diapers. I barely remember Uncle Lewis's funeral. He died just a few years after they moved to College Park. I didn't understand the full impact of his death for many years.

Since Aunt Marian's house was only one block away from my dormitory, I spent a great deal of time there during my four years of college. My friends all went away to school; I always thought I went to school in my other home town. After graduation, I moved away to start my career, but I still visited College Park, Aunt Marian's always seemed like a second home to me.

As I spent more time with Aunt Marian, she told me more about her life and her three major losses. She grew up in the rural Midwest and married young. Early in their marriage, her husband was killed in a farm accident. Aunt Marian was pregnant at the time, but two months later the baby died at birth. She told me she fell into a deep depression, so hoping a change of scenery would ease her grief, her family sent her to live with relatives in Evanston, just outside Chicago. The change in environment did wonders for her. She was soon able to find a job as a bookkeeper. Several years later, feeling more like her old self, she met Uncle Lewis. She didn't say where or how, but she did talk about how quickly she came to love him for his kindness and attentiveness. Aunt Marian's third loss was Uncle Lewis's death.

A fourth loss, though not the loss of a person's life, was in progress. As she grew older and declined in strength and mobility, Aunt Marian decided to sell the home that she loved so much and move to an apartment in an upscale retirement community a few miles away. The house sold quickly; the buyers were looking for a house close to the college. The husband was a professor there and wanted to be able to walk to work. The couple was anxious to move in, but after meeting Aunt Marian they sensitively offered to let her choose the closing date for any time within the next year.

Aunt Marian set a date far sooner than we imagined she would. I took a week off from work and traveled to College Park to help pack boxes. My sister came as well. We could tell Aunt Marian was having a tough time. She was leaving the sights, sounds, smells, and memories of the place where she had lived for so many years and where the love of her life had died. And in some ways, I think the process of moving was harder because it brought up and compounded her other losses.

Seeing that she was struggling to come to terms with the situation, I suggested that she postpone it all and ask the buyers for more time. She gave me an emphatic "No," explaining that it wouldn't be any easier a month or even a year from then. She didn't want to move, but she was determined to follow through with what she thought was best for her. So, she moved. Mom and Dad joined us on the day of the move. We thought it might be easier for Aunt Marian if she didn't have to watch her things being taken out of her house, so some friends took her to lunch and then to one of their homes for an afternoon of bridge while we supervised the movers.

For several days after my sister and I left to get back to work, Mom and Dad helped to arrange furniture and hang pictures in the new apartment.

When I visited several weeks later, I saw that they had done a beautiful job. The apartment was elegant, with two bedrooms, a large living room, a small dining room, and a small kitchen. Fortunately, Aunt Marian seemed to settle in more quickly than any of us had anticipated.

One of the saving graces of the move was Ida, who had helped Aunt Marian with her heavy house cleaning for many years. After the move to the retirement community, there was no cleaning for Ida to help with, but she drove Aunt Marian to her various appointments and helped her with errands. In addition to the services she provided, Ida's companionship was very important. Ida was always cheerful and accommodating, and I'm sure Aunt Marian compensated her generously. The arrangement gave us all a great deal of peace of mind.

Every day, Aunt Marian rose, took breakfast in her apartment, dressed neatly, and followed a schedule of social activities, reading, and watching a few television shows. She maintained a regular round of bridge parties. She took lunch and a light supper in the community dining room with the new friends she had made in the retirement community. One of us visited her nearly every weekend, even if only for a Saturday or Sunday afternoon. She never seemed lonely, but I knew that in some ways her life was full of holes: the loss of two husbands, a baby, and a home that was much more than a beautiful house.

As she became increasingly feeble, the time came when she was no longer able to leave her apartment. She had my father transfer the title of her car to Ida in appreciation of her faithful service. She engaged Ida to spend a few hours each day with her. She soon hired other caretakers as she needed more and more care. Finally, she moved into the nursing care unit. Mom, Dad, and I emptied her apartment. Although I had loved her house and been sad when the time came for her to move out, this move touched me even more deeply. I saw it as a signal of her impending demise.

Aunt Marian's minister was with her when she died three months later. It turned out that he knew her story as well as I did, and he recounted much of it at her funeral. The church was packed. The congregation was at once lifted up by stories of her generosity and determination and tearfully saddened by her death. The minister structured his homily around the various homes in which Aunt Marian lived. We found out why in his final sentence. He told us that her final words to him had been, "I know where my home will be now."

RACHEL

I suppose **I** border on indiscretion by telling the story of this particular period in my mother's life. But a new birth ought to be recorded, and **I** know my sister and our children will be better persons for this story's telling, just like I am a much better person for having witnessed it.

Papa died suddenly of a heart attack when he and Mom were in their early fifties. Both Elizabeth and I had left home for college, married, and started our own lives of family and work. Papa's death was hard for all of us, but especially for Mom. Liz and I had our families and careers, and even though we loved Papa greatly, his absence was not part of our day-to-day existence.

Mom stayed in their house, continued to work as a bookkeeper, and got even more involved in church and gardening; however, her life was not the same, not right, whatever right is. Though quiet, she had always been a caring, happy person, a kind of magnet for other people. She lived her life with the consistent and accurate approach she took to her books and figures. She said so much with so few words. All that stayed the same after Papa went away, at least on the outside. But on the inside, we all knew she was not the same, that she had lost her friend, her partner, her companion, her lover. We knew only a small part of her loss, however.

Liz and her family flew home as often as possible to see her. Since I had moved back to the area with my family, I saw much more of Mom. We were closer than she and Liz were. I think that was more a matter of physical proximity and the busyness of Liz's life.

For nearly twenty years, I watched Mom limp along with her life, staying busy, putting on her happy face. I knew, however, that she harbored a tremendous emptiness. How does one verbalize the sense of emptiness that follows nearly thirty good years of marriage? I tried to get her to talk to me about it several times, but she just brushed her feelings aside.

"Oh Melanie, I'm fine. Don't worry about me," she'd always say.

That was until about twelve years ago. Then almost suddenly I began to sense a change. She smiled more and even chuckled once in a while. Several times she reminded me of the cat that swallowed the canary. I decided to ask no questions, thinking she would tell me what was going on when she got ready.

One day, over lunch, Mom told me about Robert. She had met him at the senior center where she played bridge. He invited her to lunch after the card party. Lunch after cards became a weekly event. Then it was dinner and the symphony. They quickly became a pair. She had been seeing him for several weeks and was growing to like him more and more, but she had said nothing to anyone. Two reasons, she said. First, she felt guilty, as if going out to dinner with Robert were the moral equivalent to betrayal of her wedding vows to Papa. She had never removed her wedding ring. Second, she didn't know how Liz and I, not to mention all her church friends, would accept the fact that Robert was Jewish and active in his temple. She said that Robert was as serious about his faith as she was about hers.

I remember commenting that she seemed awfully serious about him for having known him for just two months. She just smiled, but that smile took me back to my childhood when I watched how she lit up when she was with Papa. I began to think this could be serious. And I was right on target.

On the night of her wedding rehearsal little more than six months after she had met Robert, Mom seemed as giddy as a teenager. Rabbi Silver and Father Hayton and their wives attended the dinner, as did our families and a few of the happy couple's closest friends. The food was wonderful, the toasts were thoughtful and some even funny, and the dancing was a party in itself. By the time Mom and I got back to her house—I had volunteered to spend the night with her and help with her hair and her dress the next day; she was as lightheaded as she was lighthearted.

Mom began to talk.

"Melanie, sweetie, do you know how close your Papa and I were? Well, I'll give you some hints. He turned me on like a light bulb. You and Liz saw how we loved each other."

She eased herself out of her dress and sat down on the bed, slip and hose forgotten as she clutched the dress to her breast.

She looked away but at nothing in particular. She seemed to have gone to a scene from decades past. Then she looked at me and grinned a mischievous smile.

"You didn't know your parents were full of fire for each other, sweetie. Children never want to believe their parents have sex. But, wow! We did and I loved it. Your Papa was as gentle and affectionate with me as he was to kind to you and Liz. I missed him when he was away and came alive when he returned home."

She grinned at me again, obviously aware that that I was taken back by a frankness I had never heard from her. I don't recall that she ever used the word "sex." Liz and I had gotten all our information from books and teen-talk. Furthermore, Mom and Papa were always discreet about their displays of affection. I had always sensed their warmth toward each other and how it made me feel secure as I grew up, but I wouldn't have imagined them full of fire.

Quickly, Mom seemed to switch emotions. What was such a beautiful memory gave way to a look of sadness. She stood, eased off her slip, sat down and began to remove her pantyhose.

"Melanie, for your sake, and Liz's sake, I tried hard to keep a stiff upper lip when your Papa died. I felt like an empty shell; the most important person I ever knew had left me and took a piece of my soul and body. The ache was always there. For years I reached across the bed in half sleep to touch him only to find the sheets cold on that side. I thought it would get easier, but it never did."

She unfastened her bra and let it slip down to her hands. She laid it gently on the bed and then sat down, completely naked. She seemed not to have noticed. I don't remember ever seeing her that way. But she was still beautiful, just into her seventies. Her body, for all the ravages of time, contained life, even a kind of voluptuousness.

She folded her hands in her lap and sat quietly for a minute or two. I got up from the stool at the dressing table, went to the closet, and picked out a pale blue gown. I put it around her shoulders.

"You don't want to catch cold on such an important night as this," I chided. "You're right. Thanks, Melanie," she replied quietly.

After some minutes of silence, she changed moods again. A thoughtful smile came across her whole face.

"Mel, do you remember that funny story about the travelers who visited Abraham when he and Sarah were much older than I am?"

I wasn't sure, so I didn't say anything.

"They told Abraham that Sarah would have a baby within the next year. Sarah was inside the tent and she just cackled outright. I don't blame her one bit. The kicker was her reply, probably almost to herself. She said something like, 'At my age? No such pleasure for me!' But by golly, Mel, the old woman had her pleasure and a baby too. Whaddaya think of that? And so has old Rachel her pleasure."

The next day, the wedding went off beautifully. Liz and me, spouses, grandchildren, friends of both Mom and Robert. And what a reception—it was an even fuller replay of the rehearsal dinner. A string quartet took turns with a Klezmer band. Dancing. Champagne. All of it was grand! I've never seen two people happier.

For the honeymoon, they went on a week-long cruise. Afterwards, Robert moved into Mom's house, though he kept his own house and they occasionally spent time there. Mom's house had been a somewhat neglected but was not in very bad shape. It was a Cape Cod, modest but comfortable. It always had for me the feel of a well-worn pair of slippers. The yard was a good place for my sister and me to grow up, friends always around.

Robert continued in his business but in his spare time worked enthusiastically on the house and yard, especially helping Mom with her roses in the back yard. The focus of the front yard was the big sugar maple tree. It was so beautiful every fall that passers-by often stopped to take pictures of it. When Liz and I were small, we and the neighbor children climbed in it and played under it. I remember many summer evenings, the four of us sitting in lawn chairs, drinking lemonade and talking. But like the house and Mom, it was showing its age. Robert engaged a tree service to prune the dead branches and try to save it. Afterwards, the maple seemed to take on new life, just like the couple that now lived in the house.

Robert did the same wonders with the house as he did for the maple tree. He painted inside and out, and they bought a few pieces of new furniture, including a lovely queen-sized bed. Robert's presence transformed the house and yard, just as their relationship had transformed Mom's life. The newlyweds seemed as happy as possible for more than a decade.

Then came Mom's diagnosis: aggressive cancer. She lived only five and a half months. Very little pain, but she was so weak. Robert hovered over her, cooked for her, waited on her constantly. He was always tender and affectionate. I never doubted that as Mom slipped away, a part of him went with her.

After the burial ceremonies, Robert moved back into his own house. He said that he just couldn't live there without her. We removed the best pieces of furniture and Mom's things, but Robert kept the heating and air conditioning running. He spent at least one day a week caring for the yard, especially Mom's roses. I think he did it for her. But the place was never the same; even with his devoted care, the yard was never quite as vibrant as it was when it belonged to the both of them. Perhaps it was my imagination, but even the maple tree seemed to wither with sadness.

Two years later, we experienced another loss. One cold winter night, Mom's house caught fire and burned nearly to the ground before the firefighters could extinguish the flames. I stood with my husband and neighbors as the house finally collapsed. The police later learned that some neighborhood boys and been playing in the house. Fooling around, they had tried to build a fire in the fireplace, and the fire got out of hand.

Robert had the debris cleared, but the barren lot looked a lot like a wrinkled old lady completely naked. The spring that followed brought one more loss. The maple tree had been too damaged by the heat to survive. Robert had it removed, and I could tell the process nearly undid all the healing that had taken place in his broken heart.

Robert and Liz and I talked at length about what to do with the lot. Since Mom had placed Robert's name on the deed, it was his to do with as he pleased. He offered to return it to Liz and me or to the grandchildren, but we turned down his offer. After a short time, on an occasion of Liz's next visit to settle the meager estate, Robert made a proposal to us. He offered to turn the corner lot into a little park. He wanted to plant another maple tree, keep up the rose garden, and install a couple of teak benches and a walking path for passersby. He said he would be willing to endow the lot so it would be cared for when he could no longer do the work.

We were deeply touched and agreed that he should go forward with his plan. And he did. Not at all elaborate, but its beauty and openness turned out to be a wonderful reflection of who Robert and Mom had been as a couple.

Robert became a frequent dinner guest in my home. For a long time, we had all belonged to one another through Mom, but it took only a short time for Robert to become a part of us in his own right.

Sometimes, I think I never really knew Mom until Robert caused us to see her in a new light. Their relationship helped me better understand her relationship with Papa. Each time I go to the lot and sit on one of the benches, I look at the new maple tree in the place of the old one. But it's not just a replacement; it has taken on itself a life and beauty of its own, as I suspect we all have because of a storybook love affair between Mom and Robert.

SARAH

The green Volkswagen Beetle eased around the corner, and Wallace didn't bother to change gears; he kept his foot on the clutch and let the car roll slowly past the first house.

"That's it!" exclaimed Leah. "104." She double-checked the hand-drawn map. "It's just as I pictured it: a white cottage, neat as a pin. Just like Miss Hafner."

Wallace eased the car into second gear and pulled into the driveway, stopping short of the small matching garage. He shut off the motor as Leah stuffed the map into the glove compartment and gathered her purse and the small gift she had brought. They both got out of the car and walked briskly to the door. Leah pushed the doorbell, but it scarcely had time to sound before the door opened to them.

"Well, well, well," called the pleasant lady at the door. "Right on time. Please come in."

The smiling couple entered the living room, and Miss Sarah Hafner closed the door behind them. She hugged Leah and turned to Wallace.

"And this must be Wallace," she said. "I'm so glad to finally meet you."

Wallace grinned and they shook hands.

"This is such an unexpected treat, Leah. I haven't seen you since..." Leah interrupted. "Since high school graduation. The same month you retired and moved back to Ohio."

"Yes, yes. Six years. I had no idea I would ever see you again, even though you have been so thoughtful to write to me. I have enjoyed your letters. Oh, let me look at you. So lovely. And you, Wallace. Excuse me for leaving you out. I'm so glad you're here. What a literary couple, with Leah a French teacher and you an English teacher. A fine combination, I'm sure."

Wallace and Leah beamed as Miss Hafner continued.

"Now I know you have been driving for several hours. Would you like to sit down, or would you care to stretch your legs a bit? I have tea and cookies, and I want to show you my garden, and, of course, I want to hear all about your life together. Which shall we do first?"

Leah answered, "Why don't we sit and talk? We can catch up and then see the garden, if that suits you."

"Oh yes, yes. Please make yourselves comfortable. The bathroom is just down the hall. Let me get the tea tray," Miss Hafner said as she scurried to the kitchen. Leah and Wallace sat down side by side on the Victorian sofa. They smiled at one another, and Wallace whispered, "She's just like you described her."

The living room was immaculate with everything placed precisely, tastefully, but without pretense or ostentation. Most of Miss Hafner's furniture was antique, nineteenth century in style, well cared for. Leah and Wallace would later learn that much of it had come from Miss Hafner's parents' home after they had died. A few of the pieces had belonged to her grandparents. Several old portraits and photographs hung on two of the walls. Leah had remembered from letters that Miss Hafner had no brothers or sisters, and her parents had both died in the same year not long before she had retired and moved back to Ohio.

From their seat in the living room, the couple could also see into the dining room. That room's furnishings matched the period and style of those in the living room. A sideboard occupied most of one wall and a china cabinet most of the opposite wall. Under the double window at the back of the room stood a plain, narrow table; hand-made in simple style, it provided a sharp contrast to the ornate Victorian style of most of the other furniture. The table had obviously been made or purchased with a specific function in mind: it was covered with a variety of houseplants. The lace curtains hung only across the tops of the windows, probably to allow maximum light for the plants.

While Leah looked at the old portraits and photographs on the wall, Wallace's attention was held by the details of the dining room. Its table was covered with an ivory tablecloth with a lace cloth on top. A vase of three iris blooms and two blade-like leaves stood regally in the center of the table. At the end of the table, facing the window at the back of the room and the cottage was a single place setting of china, silver flatware, and crystal. A single candle, not yet burned, in a crystal candlestick sat between the place setting and the vase of irises. The table was presided over by an old but very well cared for crystal chandelier.

A few minutes later, Miss Hafner returned to the living room with erect posture, quick steps, and an energy that belied her seventy-one years. Her confident demeanor overshadowed her slight build. Her salt-and-pepper hair was rolled and pinned at the back of her head. She wore a printed cotton housedress and a plain light blue apron. She had obviously made no effort to dress differently for this day than she did for any other. The young couple felt welcomed by her warmth and graciousness, which was more important than any arrangements or appearances.

"Here we are," she said, resting the tray on the coffee table. The tray carried a small silver tea service, three china cups and saucers, three silver spoons, three linen napkins, and a china plate of sugar cookies. Miss Hafner took a seat on the small chair across the table from her young guests. Then she began to pour the tea.

Leah poured a bit of cream into her cup. Wallace spooned sugar into her cup and then into his own. Wanting neither cream nor sugar, Miss Hafner unfolded a napkin, placed it on her knee, and took her cup and saucer in hand.

"Now the work of the hostess is done, I want to hear as much about the two of you as you have time to tell me. My, my! What a handsome couple you are! I cannot tell you how proud I am to have had a part in your life. Leah, twenty-three years ago you were a tiny thing. I carried you to your foster parents on a pillow. Oh, it was hot that day! I knew if I could get them to take you 'temporarily', I wouldn't need to find any other home for you. And how right I was! Now look at you—a schoolteacher and married!"

"You made a wonderful choice for me," Leah replied with a warm smile. "And Mother and Daddy always believed you hung the moon. We always thought I had the best social worker alive! And I was very fortunate to have them as my parents. I have always been grateful to you for that."

"Leah, about your parents; your mother died last spring, and your father still lives on the farm. Will you visit him on this trip?"

Leah talked at length about her mother's long illness and the dilemma living so far away had created. She had to honor her teaching obligations in Tennessee on the one hand while she felt that maybe she should go home and help with her mother. She spoke as well about her father and their proposal that he should come to live with them. They planned to visit Niagara Falls, drive south through central New York State, and then spend time with her father on his farm in Pennsylvania.

After a brief lull in the conversation, Miss Hafner smiled and turned to Wallace. "Let's not make this a hen party, young man. Since I know so much about Leah, please tell me about yourself."

Wallace protested that the time they had would be best invested in the two women, but he hurried through some basic facts about his life, most of which Leah had included in letters to Miss Hafner during the four years of their courtship and marriage. When Wallace seemed anxious to move the conversation back to Leah and Miss Hafner, Leah broke in with some additional information about Wallace's family, his academic interests, and his hope for graduate school. She wanted Miss Hafner to know Wallace better since he now was such an important part of who she had become.

The conversation returned to Leah and the role Miss Hafner played in her personal development as a child and teenager, Miss Hafner's retirement from the Pennsylvania child welfare department, and her move back to her home in Ohio. Miss Hafner explained how she had always intended to return to her home community and how she had purchased and furnished the house, spending her vacations and holidays there. When her parents died, she completed the furnishing process, using the things she had chosen to keep from their home.

The young couple was curious about Miss Hafner's life, but they didn't want to pry by asking personal questions. Sensing their curiosity, Miss Hafner described in summary her early career path. She felt fortunate to have been able to attend a small but academically excellent liberal arts college near her parents' farm. She had prepared herself to be a teacher in her home community, but a classmate from Pennsylvania persuaded her to move east. She immediately found a position, but not as a teacher. Her friend's father recommended her to someone in the child welfare department, and that was the only employer she ever had. After a while, Wallace broke in.

"Leah, we ought to keep an eye on the clock. We have at least three hours to drive this evening before we stop."

never enough for her to dismiss me from the job. I still don't have any talent for growing flowers, but I love looking at them."

Miss Hafner laughed and led the way out the door and into the back yard. She pointed to a nearby cottage similar to her own and told her guests that her best friend lived there. She pointed over the hedge to an area of town where her church was located. Near the church was a new community hospital.

"Everything I need is within walking distance. I hardly need to take my car out of the garage," she said. "And the exercise does me a world of good. The new hospital is one of this community's greatest assets. I can always be assured of good care, which is important to those of us who have no family except church and neighbors."

Miss Hafner led the young couple from bush to bush, plant to plant, explaining the variety and age of each one. She occasionally interrupted her explanations to mention a detail about her neighborhood, her town, or her volunteer work at the hospital. They reached the front of the house after a short walk up the slope on the opposite side of the house from the driveway.

"I wish you could spend the night with me, but I know you're on a schedule. Let's go back inside for a moment. I wrapped up some treats to sweeten your trip."

They returned to the living room, where Leah retrieved her purse while Miss Hafner went to the kitchen. Wallace's attention again was drawn to the dining room table. When Miss Hafner returned with a small paper plate covered with waxed paper and tied with white string, she noticed Wallace's interest in the dining room. She smiled at the young man, who appeared embarrassed that their hostess had caught him examining the contents of the room too closely.

"I see you are interested in my dining room table, Wallace."

"Well, I, urn.... Yes, I am, Miss Hafner. I was admiring your place-setting."

"But wondering why such an elaborate setting for one." She had moved to his side and patted his arm. "I'm pleased you noticed. May I tell you about it?"

"Certainly," Wallace replied. His interest in hearing about the dining room overshadowed his desire to get back on the road.

Miss Hafner began slowly, as if weighing just what to tell. "I left home in the mid-thirties, on my own for the first time in my life. Not many young women went to college in those days; even fewer went far from home to work. But I wanted a challenge, and my parents had always encouraged independent thought and action."

She paused and then as an aside added, "I'm not certain they wanted me to be that independent, however. But I left with their blessing." After a chuckle, she continued with her story. "Anyway, when I took the job with the child welfare department, I learned things I never knew existed, or at least did not exist as I grew up. I was idealistic; I loved the children and thought I could save every one of them. I was often moved to tears by many of the situations I encountered. I worked long hours and took paperwork home almost every night. For the first few years, the only social life I knew was through the church I joined. The friends I made were people in the church and in my office. Before I knew it, I had been there five years." Wallace looked at the place setting on the dining room table, and Miss Hafner smiled.

"Wondering what all that has to do with a single place setting on an old maid's table?" She laughed and patted his arm again. "I'll get there."

"In the early forties I began to think about my future, how long I would continue as a social worker, whether I wanted to pursue my original goal of teaching. For the first time since leaving home, I began to experience some pangs of loneliness. I began to think seriously about a home of my own. I realized I wanted to get married and have my own children in addition to my welfare children. But I had never dated anyone seriously. In fact, all my male acquaintances were part of church and work groups. To be honest, I think I had been sending non-verbal messages that I was not interested in dating, that I was too busy with my work to have time for a relationship. But inside, my thoughts for the future were making room for marriage, or at least the idea of marriage."

She hesitated. Leah moved closer to Wallace for some kind of comfort, as if she sensed something was about to be said that she did not want to hear.

Never one to miss anything, Miss Hafner said, "Yes, Leah. Something was about to happen that changed my life and the lives of millions of other people. Our country was drawn into The War, and young men from every community in the land simply disappeared on busses, trains, ships, and airplanes. Communities that only months earlier had bubbled with completely balanced populations soon experienced a shortage of young men. My interest in having a husband and children came at the exact time in history when what I wanted was least possible. This was just as well because my work in child welfare became even more important as the war placed strain upon existing families. With all that suffering, I was glad to be able to help any way I could.

"Well, the rest you can guess for yourselves. I kept myself busy with my work, fully expecting the war would be over soon and the men would return. I was only partly correct. The war lasted much longer than anyone expected, and not all the men came home. Many who did were badly wounded and troubled. Others enrolled in colleges on the G. I. Bill. So there were many fewer men in my community at that point."

"Did you consider moving to a city with a college?" Wallace broke in.

"Not for a long time," she answered. "I don't think I realized what had happened. By the time the war ended, I was in my thirties and still almost completely immersed in my work. War creates a kind of collective shock. It took a long time for all of us to understand what had happened to our country. And we experienced shock on a much smaller scale than the nations where the war was fought. Still, I had no thought of moving or changing jobs. I did find myself thinking that at the right time, whatever time that was, I would meet someone, marry him, and add family to my life.

Leah asked, "But you never married?"

"No, Leah. I did not. I never even got an offer." Miss Hafner chuckled as though this were some kind of private joke. "And when I began to realize that I probably would not marry, I decided to revise my dreams.

Wallace, this is the part of the story that includes the place-setting of china. The first thing I had to come to grips with was the possibility that for the first time in my life, I had run upon something I could not control or change. Oh, in my thirties marriage was still a possibility, but much less probable than just a few years before. But I had always been a planner, and this would be no exception. If I married, I reasoned, that would be wonderful. If I did not, I wouldn't let it keep me from enjoying my life. That life would include my own home, and this is it. It would be a life that, although alone, need not be lonely. I knew that my parents would not be with me forever, but I didn't feel that I needed to give up my independence and move home with them.

"Now the place-setting. When I decided to make the best of my life alone, I resolved never to become bitter or to give in to loneliness. Flowers and gardening became my avocation, and working with my hands in partnership with God infused my life with beauty. My second resolution was that mealtimes would always be marked for me by pleasantness. I would eat three delicious meals every. I would use my best tableware. I would have flowers and candles whenever possible. I am now in my seventies, and thankfully healthy of mind and body and positive of spirit. I entertain friends for meals occasionally, and I am invited out rather frequently. But when I eat here alone, I don't just eat, I dine.

"Well, Wallace. That's my story. I haven't told it to many people. But you are indeed a very special young man to have pulled it out of me without even asking. I hope I haven't bored you."

"Bored? Not at all." said Wallace, who had forgotten that he was the one who had reminded Leah that they needed to leave in order to keep to their travel schedule. "I feel like a most privileged person to have heard your story. And I won't forget it."

Miss Hafner smiled and turned to walk through the living room and toward the door. "Leah," she said, "one need not bear children to have children. You have given me such pleasure. Please continue to write."

Leah hugged Miss Hafner. Wallace held out his hand and pressed Miss Hafner's hand in his own. They walked to the car in silence. Leah and Wallace got into the car and drove away slowly.

Leah and Miss Hafner continued to exchange letters for nearly a decade until one evening the telephone rang. Leah answered, and Harriet Schneider identified herself as Sarah Hafner's friend in Ohio. She called to tell Leah that Miss Hafner had died after a brief illness. In her desk was a note asking that Leah be notified. The little house and its contents were to be sold, according to Miss Hafner's wishes, and the proceeds would be given to the hospital in her community.

www.ingramcontent.com/pod-product-compliance
Lightning Source LLC
Chambersburg PA
CBHW050203130526
44591CB00034B/2000